D1245227

THE
DIARY
OF A
RAPIST

OTHER BOOKS BY EVAN S. CONNELL

THE DIARY OF A RAPIST

by

EVAN S. CONNELL

THE ECCO PRESS

Copyright © 1966 by Evan S. Connell, Jr.
All rights reserved

The Ecco Press
100 West Broad Street
Hopewell, New Jersey 08525

Published simultaneously in Canada by
Penguin Books Canada Ltd., Ontario
Printed in the United States of America

FIRST ECCO EDITION, 1995

Library of Congress Cataloging-in-Publication Data
Connell, Evan S., 1924–
    The diary of a rapist / by Evan S. Connell.
      p.   cm.
    ISBN 0-88001-408-3 paperback
    I. Title
    [PS3553.05D54   1995]   94-43665
    813'.54—dc20

9 8 7 6 5 4 3 2 1

THE DIARY OF A RAPIST

JANUARY 1

Last night Bianca shook me awake and told me to stop grinding my teeth. Nothing gives her more satisfaction than to humiliate me.

So one year ends, another begins.

JANUARY 2

This afternoon on the way home from work saw three women fighting in the street. One had fallen to her knees, clothing pulled to rags. The others were jerking at her hair, hitting her furiously across the back with awkwardly closed fists. How clumsy women are! Shrieks and cries, a circle of attentive men. There's a sort of dreadful augury in the birdcall screams of women.

JANUARY 3

Violence! Violence! Had scarcely left the Bureau when I saw a man struck by a taxi—no accident. The driver noticed him start across the street, I'm sure of it, and am sure there was time enough to stop the cab. Instead, what?

5

A chance for revenge! How many of us wouldn't do the same? Yes, when that moment comes—that one instant when we've got the power either to love or hate, with nothing in between, how often do we hesitate? I know the answer. Day after day we're humiliated, so why not seize the chance? Why not?

Well, don't think about it, just do your work. Stay out of trouble. Anyway, who knows whether Love exists? It could be that Hate is the only reality. He that seeketh, findeth. Maybe. I've looked for some kind of love long enough but what have I found? Strokes of revenge, back and forth, regular as a metronome, that's what I've found. So now I ask just to be let alone. I'm willing to do my work, not much else interests me because there's not much to look forward to.

Bravo! Bravo for Earl Summerfield!—he's quite a man. Yes, get home a few minutes before your wife, rush around the apartment flinging up your hands and shouting, grin at yourself in the mirror, practice a few vulgar gestures, then as soon as you hear the elevator stop you grab the newspaper and sit down and compose your features so Bianca always comes in to find the husband she expects. Bravo, Earl, yes indeed, you're quite a man.

Well, maybe I'm too hard on myself. I doubt if other men are much better—a few, I suppose, but most of us are terrified. Scared to death of losing our job, getting in trouble with the bank, letting somebody make a fool of us. Usually it's some woman. Stiff as a dead halibut if one of them looks at us cross-eyed. The truth is I'm really no weaker than the next, not a bit & if it wasn't for Bianca I'd have been able to make something out of myself by this time. She's ruined everything. There's no limit to what I might have done by now. She knows it, too. I guess it gives her some sort of pleasure.

JANUARY 4

Friday. This noon at lunch Magnus confides that he's discovered an extremely rare paperweight. Wipes his nose, coughs, peeps around & finally lets me in on the secret. "Not many ah uh persons realize how val-val-valuable uh certain paperweights can be!" Looked at the spots of grease on his necktie & tried not to grin. Oh? Is that so? How much do you think you can get for it? Then naturally he started backing off. Wasn't sure, explained that it depended on the rarity and so forth. Claimed something called a "yellow overlay" brought $7,000. Maybe it did, I'm no authority on paperweights, but even if it did what's that got to do with Magnus? He's not going to find one that's worth anything. What he found was just an odd piece of brass and that's all he's ever going to find. A molded lump of brass in a McAllister junk shop. I'll bet he paid more than it's worth. Why does he keep on searching? Why can't he admit the truth? Why does he want to deceive himself? Mucking around at the bottom of the lake. If anything he's lower and poorer and worse off than I am. Why doesn't he admit it?

JANUARY 5

Rain. Most of my holiday on the bus riding back and forth across the city, one side to the other, listening & watching. Told Bianca I needed to get out of this apartment —no answer. Plucking a hair from her chin, lips compressed, holding the tweezers with both hands. She didn't even glance into the mirror at me. I don't know why she felt like pulling that hair, should think she'd let it grow, there's nothing she wants more than to be a man. Now that I think about it—yes! How enlightening to realize you've been deceived—eh Earl? How gratifying to discover why she married you. She's never had any interest in being a woman but at the same time there's quite a sting to spinsterhood. There must be, if it's sharp enough to make Bianca jump. Surprised I didn't realize the situation a long time ago. She's cold as a dead gull, it's that simple. I've been blind. She's never wanted to touch me—one excuse after another, I couldn't admit them to myself. I've been a fool. She's more interested in a room full of pimply, farting students than she is in me. Sweet Jesus! What a pair we make!

Excite myself too much. I've got to learn to accept things as they are. Nobody has everything he'd like to have. Oh yes, be pious—shit! I'm dying, I'm dying in this place. I'm not alive. One day like another. I could be traveling around enjoying life. Then, too, if I was in a different situation I could be making my mark on the world. I could become somebody important, have people applauding me. Radio, television, etc. My picture in the paper. Being mentioned in the gossip columns & all the rest of it. Instead, what have I got? What am I?

If I could just decide how to start getting what I want. Maybe I can figure things out on my vacation next summer. Ought to decide ahead of time where to go, get things planned. I could leave the city by myself, Bianca wouldn't care. She might not even notice that I was gone. So, that being the case, where first? Canada? England? Italy? Go to the South Seas? There's money in the bank. About $400, I think. Not exactly enough to satisfy my appetite for life, but a start. Monday get a few travel folders.

Midnight. Picking at my face again! I sit here thinking, staring out the window, then suddenly realize I'm feeling my throat & ears & nose like a blind man trying to identify a corpse.

8

JANUARY 6

Must have been out of my mind last night because the truth is that I'm not going to go anywhere, not now or ever. Not enough in the bank? That isn't the reason. Haven't got the nerve. Set down the real reason: I'm afraid. Am what I accuse others of being.

Days, weeks, months. Get up at the same time every morning, put on a suit eight years old with the elbows polished slick as oilcloth, eat poached eggs & read the Chronicle, stand like a totem pole among perfumed stenographers riding the bus downtown, then sit on a stool until 4:45 P.M. Wiggle my toes for amusement. Look down at my shoes to see if the leather's got any new cracks. Try to remember exactly how many times I've pretended to smile at the supervisor. Eh! Eh!

Caution, Summerfield. Don't count the past.

JANUARY 7

Just fixed myself a bowl of soup, it didn't sit well on my stomach. Don't know what time it is, but late. Bianca's asleep, grateful for that. Stopped at the bedroom door & listened to her breathing. Why did I marry the old lioness? She's already 33, here I am just 26. I'm still young and she's middle-aged. "We're not children any longer, Earl." Certainly lets me know, means more than it says, turns me away subtly. Oh she's clever, closes everything up tight as a safety pin. "Earl in the name of sense stop acting like a child!" What am I expected to say? Turn my face aside? Apologize? She's smarter than I am & I lose every argument, but that doesn't mean she'll win. I'm not weak. I know I'm not.

JANUARY 8

Newspaper item says some housewife in Chicago was tied up, painted with tar and then set on fire. Burned like a torch. Nobody could get close to her. People could hear her screaming even though the tar was bubbling across her mouth. Makes me think of those women fighting in the street. I keep seeing that one on her knees with her blouse torn and the white boobs spilling out—dangling like pendulums in a surrealist painting.

What else? Weather report calls for clouds & probable rain. My head feels squashy, afraid I might be catching cold.

JANUARY 9

Typical day at the Bureau. Mrs. Fensdeicke continually wiping her lips with a lace handkerchief while she glides around behind our backs, clipboard nestled like an unborn baby in her arms. Marks down her observations, smiles. "Please continue with your interview, Mr. Summerfield." I should be used to it by now. If only I knew what she was writing about me. One day I'll ask to have a look. Yes. Then her lips would turn into a pink pincushion and pat-pat with the handkerchief, smile to show she's aware of the joke. She's sick so I shouldn't be so critical. Of course that overhead light does make every one of us look like a mummy, but am positive she's ill. Bugs inside nibbling nibbling. Less and less of Mrs. Sara Fensdeicke. I guess I ought to feel sympathetic but the fact is I don't. I'm worried that one of these days she's going to accidently touch me with her shred of lace, then I'll do something awful, God knows what. Kick her. Strangle. The way she holds that handkerchief for some reason reminds me of Bianca holding a cigarette—yesterday—no, day before it must have been—at dinner, had to shut my eyes. I think it's certain mannerisms of women that make us want to kill them.

JANUARY 10

Thursday, Thursday, Thursday! What a tedious year this will be. Scarcely past Christmas holidays but already I look forward to vacation. Waiting for the bus this evening & noticed people staring at me, realized I was crumpling the newspaper. Forced to grin & make an excuse. Said out loud that I was tired of reading about nothing except corruption, murder, war. Nobody answered. Tempted to shout at them. "Are you deaf?" Don't they know what's going on? Gets worse every day but they go right on just as they always have, pay no attention. However, I guess underneath they're as worried as I am, all of us hoping for improvement of one sort or another. Fensdeicke, for instance, worried about lungs or whatever it is, Magnus wandering around in search of the rainbow. Vladimir and his worn-out Bolshevik reforms, fifty years late. Old Clegg wanting nothing to change, absolutely Nothing! Pins & decorations on his lapel disgust me. McAuliffe must hope for something—more women, more liquor, that's about all. At lunch today almost thrust my fork into his eyes when he kept talking about the women he's had in Auckland, Port Said, etc. All right, he's been to Faraway Places, had experiences I'll never have, but what's that got to do with it? He wastes his experiences, wastes his entire life! So why should I concern myself with him or anything he talks about?—he's insignificant. Filthy. Filthy in body as well as in mind. Dirt under his

11

fingernails, obscene jokes. He makes me sick. It's an irony that we're doing the same work, considering how much difference there is between us.

Well, I don't know why I allow thinking about McAuliffe to upset me, particularly when I realize that before long I'll be getting somewhere and he won't ever. He gives me the impression that he's rotting away inside. His liver must be gone, eyes watery as eggs. Disintegrating. So I suppose I ought to be grateful. Even if his liver does hold up he's not going to amount to anything, always be what he is right now —Interviewer, State Employment Bureau—lowest possible classification. One grade above File Clerk. Magnus, Vladimir, old Clegg & McA & I in the same basket, all five of us perched on stools, 5 in a row. I'm the only one who doesn't belong.

JANUARY 11

Today being Friday treated myself to a drink downtown after getting off work. Chatted quite a while with a wealthy man from New York who's out here to open a branch of his investment business. Let him know I might be interested in joining the firm, made certain he caught my name. There's no telling, he might call. I believe I made a good impression. Pretended I'd given out all of my cards. I think I ought to have some cards printed up.

JANUARY 12

So much violence that nobody pays attention to it any more. Old man on Potrero Hill beaten to death last night by gang of boys in painted leather jackets. Negro woman in Menlo Park stabbed so many times they just called it death from "multiple" wounds. Another woman's body dredged up from the bottom of a lake in Trinity County, hands & feet tied. Oakland choir boy, honor student, president of his class, etc., got his throat cut while walking home through a vacant lot. What else? Well, Archbishop somebody-or-other got his picture in the paper tonight—blessing the cornerstone of a new church. Makes me sick. Feel like keeping track of everything, then throwing it into the face of the next person I meet.

Shouldn't get angry like this. Look out for myself, let others do the same.

Don't know why am so depressed. Last argument with Bianca? Always accepting blame as if I was her servant. Six years in these dirty rooms, circling each other like dogs. Six years! Telling myself tomorrow something will happen to improve the situation but it never does. No wonder we don't have any friends. Other couples keep out of our way, I don't blame them. Not much happiness here. A bent coin, Earl & Bianca.

JANUARY 13

Day of leisure. B spent half of it reading poetry to herself, then back to grading papers & now she's gone to some concert with Spach. As if I didn't know what she's up to! Not satisfied to be teaching mathematics, wants some sort of executive position where she'll have more authority. She'll get it. Sooner or later Spach's going to feel obligated without really knowing why and will see that she gets whatever she wants. I don't care. Let her become principal of the rotten school, no business of mine. Don't care what she does.

So here you sit again, Earl Summerfield. Sunday night to yourself! Prowl the apartment, suck at your fingertips, contemplate yourself in the bathroom mirror—bulging forehead and puckered lips. Why do you look so worried? Walk to the back porch again, stare at the lighted windows across the alley. Dancing figures, a mandolin, Italian arguments. You're dry with envy, Earl. That's so. Others are living life, you're only watching.

I don't deny it. Well, then. Hmm. I wonder how it would be to move to Europe, take a cottage on a hillside above the Adriatic. Live surrounded by pigs and goats and a dozen children and odors of hay and manure. Hmm!

Dear Jesus before much longer I'll become a creature of fads & fancy. Lights will come to seem too strong or weak, every day too cold or warm, and acquaintances impossible. I don't have any friends as it is, want none. Next year at this time I'll demand more sugar, suffer headaches, trace my thoughts like tendrils of convolvulus, yes, and sit in a wooden chair cracking my finger joints while I wait for supper.

Bitter depths. Bitter depths.

JANUARY 14

Felt drowsy after getting home from work, grateful Bianca wasn't here. Awoke instantly to the noise of her key in the lock, my expression suitably alert, suitably neutral. She has no idea who I am. Years arch over our heads, yet Bianca continues to think that I am what I used to be.

Earl Summerfield! she cries—EARL SUMMERFIELD! Is that what you do? Sleep? Is that all you do?

Have no idea what time it is, clock's stopped. It must be late & I still hear the echoes of her voice.

JANUARY 15

This noon an attack of vertigo. Thought I'd fall. Managed to lie down, absolutely humiliated. To have people staring down at you—forced to admit in public that you're sick—can't remember when I've been so embarrassed. It gave everybody the impression that I'm not in very good health. I can't imagine what happened today. And the worst of it was McAuliffe acting cynical, could tell from his grin that he thought I was malingering. He's gotten afternoons off with various pretenses & so assumes other people are equally dishonorable. It's as if he regards conscientious people as being foolish. The thought of him nauseates me. Reminds me of a diseased stork with its feathers dropping out, greasy hair dangling over those bloodshot eyes. A person could die and he'd think it was a trick. I'll ignore him tomorrow, won't say good morning. If I'm indebted to anybody in that office for consideration it's Mrs. Fensdeicke, and am forced to admit to myself it's a surprise. Would never have guessed she could be so solicitous, but then she's a woman. Illness touches them every time. One of the few things I like about them. She wanted to call a doctor. Perhaps I should have agreed instead of getting to my feet. Still felt dizzy, but lying down in public was unbearable & not one person in that office will ever forget what happened today. I hate them for seeing me helpless, even though the fault was mine. How awful, the whole business. Worries me. Never had an attack like that before. Mr. Foxx came out and looked at me lying on the couch. I felt like such an idiot, nodding and smiling although he didn't say a word. Somehow that moment changed our whole relationship. I remember staring up at that puffy brown face—he looked older, too, noticed the gray hair—I think he's West Indian or Puerto Rican. Tempted to speak to him as an equal but didn't quite have courage. Should have let him know I'm too intelligent to be doing the work I'm doing. Yes, there was your moment, Earl! Why didn't you seize it? However, I have a feeling that he understood. He may very possibly be considering me for a supervisor's position. We're one short, rumor is. I could be the appointee. I've taken examinations enough, so Something ought to come of them. Foxx could do a great deal for me. I only wish I'd made a better impression. I wonder what he saw when he looked down—Summerfield lying on the maroon leather couch with a wool blanket pulled up to his chin and his feet sticking out. I could feel a draft on my ankles. What a day to be wearing these dime-store socks—it was all I could do to prevent myself from explaining I bought just one pair almost as an amusement because they were inexpensive. Ordinarily nobody would notice but I had to choose this particular day to get sick and expose them to the world. Oh God. I hope Mr. Foxx didn't notice them. He must have. Yes, they did turn out to be an amusement, they certainly did! Well, too late now, too late to fret. Went back to his office without a word. I expected him to give me the remainder of the day off. Seems rather odd he didn't suggest it. Even so he's a good man. He's all right. Whatever he wants me for—anything at all! I've thought of him as somebody to avoid. Do your work, keep out of the chief's way, that was my motto, but now I think I've been too self-effacing. Much too much. He's aware of me now. I could drop by his office on the way out some evening and mention the incident, thank him for his consideration, shake hands. We might have lunch together some day. Yes, that might not appear strange. I'm sure there's no regulation against it. Why shouldn't we become friendly? I ought to let him have a closer look at me. It's foolish to be humble.

16

JANUARY 16

Felt much improved today, quite cheerful in fact. My steps were brisk. I was the model civil-service employee marching from desk to filing cabinet and back again. Displayed my most seriously efficient look. Have decided to impress Mrs. Fensdeicke. There, that's the spirit, Summerfield Call me Horatio. Yes, Mrs. F—check-check-check like a chicken scratching at your clipboard and no Mrs. F! Eight hours of it! What was my reward? Now, what the Bureau is seeking to achieve in our particular area, Mr. Summerfield, is what Mr. Foxx often refers to as—heh! heh!—a machine-like rapidity. "Indeed?"—that's what I should have answered, instead of smiling. Why do I always act so obsequiously? What have I to fear? How much longer am I to put up with these insults? There's beauty imprisoned beneath the surface of our world and if anyone's to find it that person will be Earl Summerfield.

JANUARY 17

McAuliffe's latest tidbit: the celebrated Bird Nest Soup. Made out of the nests of the sea swallow, he claims, and has a strong taste, like crayfish soup. The nests are built from seaweed and the leaves stuck together by the spawn of fish, which is extremely rich in phosphorus, and everybody knows, says he, that phosphorus is an erotic stimulant. Eat too much, he says, and it'll poison you! Small danger of that. What won't he think of next? Half his life has been spent wallowing in dreams of sex, money for liquor and pornographic books. I wonder where he gets them. Mexico, he says, winks & smiles. He buys them somewhere in this city.

17

That pack of cards he showed me during lunch—lost my appetite. No, not true. I'm pretending once again. I went right on eating. But there was a reason—Mrs. Fensdeicke not six feet away! If she'd so much as glanced at us she'd have seen them. McAuliffe handed them to me so casually she never noticed. Still, that's not surprising, now that I consider it. Women seldom realize what goes on about them.

JANUARY 18

McAuliffe says Mr. Foxx has a white mistress young enough to be his granddaughter. I don't believe it. Told McAuliffe it was a lie. He grinned and shrugged. How would he know?—even if it was the truth, which it isn't. He couldn't know. It's just that he's filthy himself. He's vile and wants to smear slime on decent people. There are not many people I believe in any more, but I do believe in Mr. Foxx. He's a good man.

I have a feeling all of us need to believe in somebody, maybe it doesn't matter who. Also I think it doesn't make much difference what we are, weak or contemptible, we can change. Can become what we were intended to be. Yes, I do believe this and if it makes me an optimist—all right, that's exactly what I am!

JANUARY 19

Another dog poisoned in the neighborhood last night—five so far this month. Humanity isn't much to be proud of. Thugs on the loose assaulting people so the streets aren't safe any more, etc. You'd think the police would do something, but they'd rather write out traffic tickets.

Burned the note, have no intention of making a fool of

myself. Citizens don't count, not if you're entrenched at City Hall. They'd just laugh at me. I realize how unimportant I am—oh yes, oh yes! Here's a letter from Earl Somebody complaining about dogs being poisoned. Throw it away. The Mayor's got more important problems. That's what would happen, no point fooling myself that anybody in an important position would listen to me. Earl Nobody.

JANUARY 20

Ugly Sunday, my own fault. For some reason I won't let myself forget last Christmas. Almost a month gone by but still worrying it like a half-dead mouse. $20 from my wife, right out of her purse during breakfast, didn't even bother to slip it into a gift card. "Earl, I've been too busy to go shopping. Buy yourself whatever you want." At least she might have said "Merry Christmas!" But oh no, even that would be an effort. She treats me like a child who's always in the way. Should have jammed the money in her mouth. Well, I did next best—wasted it. Two pounds of chocolates. Sweater I don't want or need, also a couple of books I probably won't read, stuffed the last two dollars in somebody's mailbox. I trust your Christmas was equally pleasant, my precious wife! If you care to know the truth I spent a good many hours selecting that robe. Do you ever plan to wear it?

On & on, over & over! Forever abuse myself.

JANUARY 21

Looks like we've got a lunatic in the building. He threatened me again today. I think he lives on the 2nd floor. 201. 206. I'll see if I recognize his name on the mailbox.

Have noticed him several times but paid no attention—cropped hair, stubble on his jaw, yellow canvas jacket, dirty trousers, makes me think he might be an ex-convict. That slack once-muscular little body—he could be dangerous. Glared at me, gesticulated, pretended he was going to spit. I suppose I was a bit contemptuous but he was the one who spoke first. I'll keep on as I have, do everything possible to avoid him. Remember last week at the laundry I hopped out of his way, wondering if I'd get a blade in my ribs. He swaggers around with hands in his pockets, no way of guessing what he's up to. Wonder if I ought to mention it to the police. It's none of my business, I'd better keep quiet. Besides, they could ask what he's actually done, then what would I answer? Well, I'd be forced to admit that so far he hasn't actually Done much of anything, as far as I know he hasn't. Just that he's threatening & I have this feeling he's dangerous. Don't know how I know, but have no doubt. It's beneath the surface. Why is he challenging me? I think I should go to the police. Imagine. Harrumph! You tell us he's insane? WHY is he insane? So there I'd be. Trapped, not able to say a word, having thrown suspicion on myself. Maybe the best solution is mind my own affairs, keep away from him & make sure he understands he'd better not push me around. I think that's how to handle it. Ignore his presence, don't even look at him if we meet in the corridor. Be careful not to turn my back on him, watch him from the corner of my eye.

Otherwise today? Tum-tum-te-tum very very little. Cloudy but didn't rain. Sick of winter. Shouldn't complain so much, we never have to worry about icy streets and so forth as the rest of the country does. Then of course the summer's always cool. Count your blessings.

JANUARY 22

What a dull dull Tuesday. Has anybody on earth ever been as bored as Earl Summerfield? Impossible! I suppose I'm feeling all right, but continue concerned about that Spell a few days ago, whenever it was. Let's have a look. Week ago today! Doesn't seem possible, time slipping out from under my feet. I just wonder how much longer I can go on like this, especially because of the relationship with B deteriorating. Seems like we don't have much in common any more. If I came back to a good meal and—well, came back to what I have a right to expect, then I wouldn't mind the job every day. But there's nothing for me at the office, nothing for me here. Don't know what I want, just feel as if I'm drowning. Tomorrow the water will rise a fraction of an inch higher. Can almost see it rising from the floor, submerging the office while I sit there conducting interviews. Fill out these papers and come back at two o'clock, report to Mr. Rostov at the next window, he'll take care of you, my man, he'll take care of you at two o'clock. Then the next & next. How long out of work? Name of previous employer? How long in that position? Reason for discharge? Applied previously for compensation? Married? How many children? How many years of school? Can you drive a truck? Well, I'm tired of it all! Tired of their stories, tired of the cheats and lies. I know what they're going to say. "My wife she's sick, Mister. She got some kind of bone disease. Oldest boy, Rafe, he broke his arm last week. My father, he died in Tuscaloosa a little while back. The doctor, he says I ought not to do this work no more, the dust is bad on my lungs. Don't know what we're going to do. Rain put me out of work, Mister. The foreman, he laid off twelve of us, you can ask him. I ain't lying. Won't be nothing for at least a month.

I'm willing to do anything. Except my lungs, Mister, I'm—"
One right after the other. Next. Next. Step up to the yellow
line, wait there until your number is called. So they wait and
I wait, all of us wonder how much longer. File clerks scurrying back and forth opening drawers, squatting down, inviting everybody in the office to look at their hams—well,
they'll get what's coming to them! Goggle-eyed laborers staring, whispering to each other. I know what's going on. Dogs
that come to lick the sores of a beggar. Which is more disgusting?

JANUARY 23

Feel better tonight, not so angry. The fact is, I
feel sorry for most of the people I know. I pity them. Magnus, for example, living with his sister and brother-in-law,
one little room, a cheap radio for company. Last week telling me about an Arkansas farmer who plowed up a diamond weighing almost two carats. Asked if he was going to
start plowing up his back yard. He didn't laugh. Serious and
humble as a cur he says his brother-in-law wouldn't allow it.
Now he's convinced he knows where to find one of the jeweled Easter eggs that belonged to the Czar! Heard about
some antique shop in the suburbs where somebody noticed
this thing on sale for five dollars. "It's worth a f-fortune! An
enormous f-f-fortune!" No doubt, no doubt. So he spends
half his lunch hour quizzing Vladimir. Vladimir, what happened during the Revolution? Vladimir shakes his head.
Barely remembers Mother Russia. He was in Belgium, so he
claims, and as for the Czar's playthings he doesn't know any
more about them than I do. There's one in some antique
shop around here? Yes, yes, and you can have it for five
dollars. Oh well, finish the dream, Magnus. Soon enough

22

you'll be two dim lines near the back of the Chronicle, that's your fortune. But go ahead, Magnus. Dream of the afternoon you'll discover locked in the dust and darkness of half a century the toy of an emperor. Imagine the egg, Magnus, studded with rubies and emeralds, with a solid gold hasp, and inside the egg?—on a black velvet cushion a sapphire as blue as the Caspian Sea! Oh yes. Of course. Let us know when you find the treasure of the Czar. As for myself, I regard the entire world as an illusion from which each man must free himself in order to find Salvation.

JANUARY 24

I'm more alive at the Bureau than here—this apartment's lifeless. We should move. But where? Unless you've got money these buildings are all alike. How would it be with a fine view of San Francisco bay? A doorman in a blue uniform and a cap who'd greet me whenever I went out or in. He'd press a gold button and the elevator doors would slide apart. The corridors wouldn't stink. Yes, Stink is the word. That lunatic below us pees on the carpet, I'm sure of it, no mistaking the odor. Tomorrow I'll ask Bianca.

JANUARY 25

The Brazen Head has spoken. Sweet Christ in Heaven, are there other men obligated to live as I do—restricted everywhere by women?

I doubt if she was even listening to what I said, went on reading the financial page. I should have made a sarcastic comment. Has First Charter gone up today? Good earnings report, no doubt. Rumors of a merger, excellent, excellent!

23

Why don't you open an office, Bianca? You have the heart and soul of a broker. Bianca Summerfield. Stocks & Bonds. Member New York Exchange.

Have I begun to hate her? Yes, I have. God help us both. And yet this isn't what I wanted. This isn't what I expected.

JANUARY 26

Saturday. Bianca tutoring all afternoon. Two schoolgirls in baggy sweaters, sleeves pushed up to the elbow, the current fad. They stared at me, I stared right back until they dropped their eyes—the most satisfaction I've had this year. Was very anxious to stay in the front room so I could look at them. Bianca guessed it, asked if I wasn't going out for a walk. She's so delicate. Didn't want them to understand why she wanted me out. So I said that I was about to leave—giving it the right emphasis, suggesting I might not come back. She just shrugged and looked bored, obviously doesn't care if I live or die. So put on my jacket and went out. I should have said something to the girls as I went by the table. Hoped they'd glance up from their books but suspect they were afraid to. Don't know why I despise them. They act so innocent but then something turns up in the papers like last week where one of these little innocents was "taken into protective custody" because police discovered she was earning about a thousand dollars a week between the time she got out of school and the time she came home for supper. Found a shopping bag stuffed with money in her school locker and a pillow case full of dollar bills hidden in her closet at home. Money everywhere! The little pig was rolling on her back squealing with pleasure every afternoon in somebody's apartment or hotel room, earning more in five minutes than I make by working all day. Yes, but if you'd see her at school you'd assume she was a sweet little girl. Same as those two Bianca tutors. They're probably up to the same tricks. Well, if I had them here right now in this room I'd teach them something they'll never learn from B. No urge to sleep. Have got myself upset again by thinking about this afternoon. Now what? Sit here until dawn? I've done that too often. Lights twinkling on the bridge. See if I can get some music on the radio. Not able to sit still. Can't quit thinking.

JANUARY 27

So much for trying to apologize to Bianca! I was a fool to bring up the subject, also shouldn't have asked if they were coming back next Saturday. Dirty bitches.

JANUARY 28

Monday. Rumor about us having a second supervisor has started up again. Supposedly the first of the month. If true it means I'm being passed over because I'd certainly be informed by this time. Ought to find out how these matters are decided because I'm convinced there's more to it than examination scores. You need influence in order to get ahead. Old Clegg so many years at that same wicket, same classification. No reason for me to go on and on like that. I'm intelligent and ambitious, plenty of good qualities, so should be promoted. My main problem is getting to know people, get acquainted with them. Usually I have an impression they talk about me after I leave. They think I'm conceited, perhaps, when just the opposite is the case. It's my expression.

Anyway, the key to my particular situation must be Mr. Foxx. All right, get acquainted with him. Make an effort to do so. Find a reason to visit his office. Also, as a matter of general principle: Quit Wasting Time. Bring yourself into focus, decide who you are & what you wish to become. Do you want to spend 20 years on a stool like Clegg and wear a paper flower? Join the American Legion or Elks Club and collect postage stamps? Get mixed up in Vladimir's socialistic jargon? It's easy to wait around thinking the situation's going to resolve itself. Or go on pretending like Magnus that one day you'll find a treasure in a box. No, thank you. No, no, no! I'm not going to let myself be deluded.

So forth and so forth until the rainbow cracks, shatters, comes tinkling to the ground. Don't feel well just now. Not even positive where I am. My name sounds odd. Lightheaded. Maybe I ought to rest awhile. Remember reading how some famous man wrote to his mother that he had everything a human being could desire—a life in which he could exert himself and Grow day by day, in fine health, without passion or confusion, without troubles or agitation, like a man beloved of God who's completed ½ of his existence and who because of past suffering has been tried in preparation for future suffering. If only life was that simple for me! I'll make plans but they won't work out. Hopes snap like sticks. What else should I expect? With nothing at the start how could I have less when everything's finished? No answer. Nothing except silence.

JANUARY 29

Profile bad. Chin watery. I'd look more forceful with a beard, but of course would lose my job. Not one man at the office with a beard. Mr. Foxx has a small mustache, also a couple of men on the second floor, and Vladimir. I have a feeling Fensdeicke wants to make V shave it off. I wonder if he knows. I wonder if she'll suggest it to him. Pos-

26

sible. He's afraid of her and she knows it. So far she hasn't dared, but I think she will. Smile, remark how nice he'd look without his mustache, shifting the clipboard from one arm to the other so he can't miss the threat. After that she'd like to cut off his balls. I just wonder if he knows. He doesn't say much. I admire his courage. Maybe next year I'll grow a mustache. Think it over. Don't want people laughing at me.

I spend too much time looking in the mirror—positive indication of failure. I should learn to Act, worry less about my appearance. I have a good reputation, conscientious, always pleasant, never curl my lip at anybody. Too much so. People think of me as a vegetable, assume I don't mind the abuse. They think I'm not aware of the hurts, the insults, everything else. But I realize how I'm being treated. Oh yes.

JANUARY 30

International police working undercover have reports of worldwide ring of exotic prostitutes. Apparently there's an elaborate brochure with descriptions & photos of the Merchandise. All you need is a thousand dollars cash & then just take your pick. Fly to Hamburg or Trieste or Copenhagen or anywhere on earth and do whatever you feel like doing. That's how some people live. They get a taste of life that Earl Summerfield won't ever know a thing about. But why not? Why can't I live like that? Bianca's the only woman I ever had. She used me. Got what she wanted. I hardly enjoyed it even at first. Didn't much enjoy kissing her—lips too thin. Remember the first time I kissed her being surprised by the hard, closed teeth. I guess I've never impressed her very much. If I was important she might be different. Too late now. Caught in this uninteresting life. Caught.

27

JANUARY 31

Quite a discussion at lunch about the latest crime. McAuliffe claims to know a detective who told him she was tied to a chair in a peculiar position so the first thing police saw when they broke into the apartment was It. The things that happen between their sex and ours, impossible to believe. Guess we don't belong together. Or do we?

Half hour wasted imagining. Police take pictures of those crimes, keep them on file, McAuliffe might be able to obtain permission for us to have a look. But if he did I wouldn't go. I'd be ashamed.

Why does he like to talk about them? Why do I listen? I feel like vomiting but I always listen. Last Tuesday at lunch talking about that medical student going back to the room where there was a post-mortem, pulled aside the sheet and climbed on the table. Same as if she was asleep says McA. If a woman's asleep or dead she doesn't judge you, no need to be afraid.

Past midnight. B's probably asleep by now. If I slipped in cautiously—perhaps.

FEBRUARY 1

Celebration being planned for Washington's Birthday. Parade to start in North Beach, ending at Aquatic Park, where they're going to have speeches plus a big program of entertainment including appearances by a former governor, several Hollywood actors, folk-dance group, high-school band that won the state tournament, etc., etc. I guess the chamber of commerce must be sponsoring it. Emphasis seems to be on patriotism as well as other qualities that have made America great. Admit to feeling a bit cynical considering what happens every day. Read the paper, listen to newscasts, choose your own examples. Another abortion death in the Tenderloin, police picked up a bartender who they think did it. She didn't have enough to go to Mexico or Sweden or wherever the rich ones go to get it done. Drug addicts everywhere, pretty soon we'll have more than China. Or take that old man they caught molesting children —64 years old the paper says but he looks twice that. Stains on his vest, suit rumpled, alcoholic if I'm any sort of judge. Probably never amounted to much, not even when he was young. Guess he's trying to remember Youth before he dies. They say he breaks into fits of weeping but otherwise doesn't show much sign of regret, in fact hardly knows why they're keeping him in jail. He wants to go home. Scratches his grizzled cheek & looks puzzled. They're thinking about moving him to a different jail because of the mob outside—people frothing at the mouth they're so anxious to lynch him. Looks to me like one unimportant old man all by himself has thrown an awful scare into every bloody mother's son. As if by killing him—oh well, what's it to me! The country's stuffed as full as a baked lobster with the turds of Greatness. No business of mine, here it is Friday night, the weekend coming. I ought to be deciding how to enjoy myself. Soon enough the cycle starts again.

Five minutes ago Bianca knocked at the door. That noise is like a needle shot into my brain. She does it on purpose. Always has an excuse, needs to talk to me about something when actually she's just exasperated because I'd rather sit here by myself than do whatever it is she wants me to do. Bothering me gives her quite a lot of satisfaction, but if she had any idea what thoughts come into my head on account of it she'd quit. The celebrated intuitions of women are a myth, nothing but a courtesy we've granted them. If she keeps doing that I'll cut her into 67 pieces and have myself a shishkabob. Suck the marrow of her bones just as she's sucking at my soul.

Ho hum! Guess I might attend that Aquatic Park show on the 22nd. It could be worth seeing and I'll be in a better mood.

FEBRUARY 2

Saturday's ended. Those two schoolgirls were here, ugly scene I don't want to think about. Put it out of mind, Earl. It's over. Won't happen again.

FEBRUARY 3

Dozed awhile this afternoon and dreamed I was standing on the edge of a high building with huge crowd below—everybody waiting to see whether I was going to jump or fall or be saved. A priest and a police officer were trying to stop me from jumping. The motive of the policeman was clear enough, and he didn't bother to disguise his indifference about what happened to me, just told me to get down off the ledge and nobody would hurt me. But I remember being suspicious of the priest. God loves you—that's what I heard him say. "What God? What God?" I answered. Then he opened his mouth and spoke again, but he didn't say a word.

Well, Earl, apparently you didn't jump, you lived through one more day—for whatever it's worth. It wasn't worth much. Foggy & cold, even now. And tomorrow's not apt to bring surprises.

FEBRUARY 4

Shows how wrong you can be! This A.M. on the way to work I found $5. I thought it was a trick. Saw the bill lying in the gutter at the corner of Van Ness. It looked as bright as the moon but I walked several more steps with eyes straight ahead thinking some people around there were waiting to laugh at anybody who tried to pick it up. Then stopped and casually rubbed my jaw, glanced back, nobody paying any attention, so I just walked over and picked it up and calmly walked away. Scared to death, expecting a hand on my shoulder every instant. Twenty-six years and I guess this is about the first luck I ever had. Should be pleased—

finding $5!—but I'm not. At first I was excited, could hardly keep from dancing. Not now. $5 worth of luck.

FEBRUARY 5

Tomorrow and tomorrow and tomorrow until the end of recorded time! Simple promises accepted by simple men. What an imbecile I am to accept this life. Yes Earl, honestly how do you like it? How do you like knowing that every single one of them—even the stupidest—even those that can't so much as sign their own name!—how do you like knowing every one of them earns more money than you do? The ones with a 3rd grade education, Earl, they earn 18% more per hour than you do. Well, maybe you'd better take another look at yourself Mr. Summerfield! What do you intend to do about it? Complain to Mr. Foxx?

Why do I goad myself!—not a thing in the world I can do. Not a thing. I was so positive I'd be climbing right up through the ranks of the Bureau, positive that by this time I'd have an office of my own with a private secretary. Five years ago I thought I'd be on a level with Foxx by now, the truth is I haven't advanced a step. Don't understand it. I conduct more interviews than anybody else in the department—Fensdeicke told me so. Also, very few errors. This information must be on record somewhere, therefore why don't they promote me? Suppose that in fact I could speak to Foxx about it. Perhaps all that's necessary is bringing the matter to somebody's attention. He could write a memo to whoever his superior is in Sacramento. Certainly wouldn't do any harm. My career's at a standstill, to say the least. I'm being wasted. Maybe the Bureau's just too big. People can often be overlooked no matter how efficiently they perform, or how badly. Well, I might just throw a rock through the front window and wait to see if that has any effect—doubt if it would. Sometimes get the feeling I could pick up a gun and shoot Fensdeicke dead on the spot, it would be noted on one of the files and that would be the end of the matter. Waiting for summer. Long way off.

FEBRUARY 6

Vandals got into a house on Geary street last night, not far from here. Owner out of the city. Neighbors reported lights, noises, police discovered most of the furniture broken—sawed to pieces, hacked, mattresses ripped apart, mirrors shattered, paint poured into the washing machine, dishes thrown against walls, lighting fixtures pulled out, carpets burned & cut, shoes & garments stuffed into the toilet, bathtub filled and overflowing, etc. Pictures in the morning Chronicle, everybody astonished. At lunch old Clegg shaking his head over it. If he had his way he'd line them up against the wall and call out the firing squad, teach them a lesson. Fensdeicke agreeing, saying it's "simply dreadful!" She can't understand how people can behave like that. All I could do to keep from laughing.

FEBRUARY 7

Beginning to think we've gotten to be the most savage nation on earth. Not so peaceful and charitable and decent as we claim. Oh no, not quite! Magazine article reports we have 10 times as many murders per capita as England, 9 times as many rapes as Italy, 8 times as many thieves as there are in France. Doesn't surprise me, I've sensed it. Merely walking along the street I've sensed America's savage soul. A thousand explanations, but the fact remains.

FEBRUARY 8

Tempted to keep a scrapbook of monstrous events. Abominations in the sight of the Lord. No end to the examples. This A.M. a man on his way to work stopped by car filled with boys who hit him with tire chains, gouged out one of his eyes, drove away laughing and clapping their hands. Here I sit thinking about it while Bianca calmly studies stock-market reports. Fills me with disgust. In the Book of Tobit they say I used to do many acts of charity for my brothers. I would give bread to the hungry and my clothes to the naked, and if I saw one of my people dead and thrown outside the wall of Nineveh, I would bury him. Oh yes, but that was in the time of Shalmaneser, and I'm different now. How different I am! Weigh my iniquities as well as those of every other inhabitant of the earth—weigh them on scales and which way the movement of the pointer turns will be found out! Disgust is the least word I could use. Spit out the word. I shut my eyes & spit on whoever's convenient. That's how it is. No bread to the hungry, clothes I keep for my own use. Let the dead rot in the open city! Yes. And worse. Well, somebody—who? no matter—made a bet with friends, went to a brothel and there in front of them all he got on a whore without taking the hat off his head or taking the cigar out of his mouth. More than a crude boast about virility. Must have been his way of announcing contempt for whatever society holds sacred. Of course there are other ways of proving it. Anyhow, sooner or later we come together side by side, toes pointing stiffly at the sky.

FEBRUARY 9

Glad this day is done! Robin & Twinka here most of the afternoon hunched over their books on the dining-room table. I wasn't able to keep away from them. Knew there was going to be trouble, couldn't help myself. Promised myself I would watch television, keep my back turned to them, keep out of the dining room, but heard their voices and my good intentions weren't worth a gumdrop—sneaking to the door holding my breath, on my knees as low as I could get. They knew I was there. Cocking their legs apart —the dirty sluts. But naturally they pretended not to know anything about it when B came after me. So it's my fault. I'm to blame, who else! I'm always to blame. As far back as I can remember I've been to blame for whatever happened.

Just now occurred to me they must have told her. Of course, otherwise B wouldn't have noticed. So they did it deliberately, encouraged me—yes, now that I think about it. So they think they can make a fool of me! Well, they're going to pay for that. I won't forget. I'll get even with them, yes, and then some, don't care how long it takes. I'd like to tie them up tight together, give them a taste of the candle.

I think I could be quite a teacher. Quite a teacher.

FEBRUARY 10

Sunday afternoon and I've been out walking, am now downtown in a Market Street coffee shop. Few minutes after 5 P.M. Have a nice table to myself in the corner and can look out at the street. The window's fly-specked and coffee is not very good but I don't care, am feeling cheerful. Buttery shafts of light slanting between empty office build-

35

ings. I'm sitting here among people who don't amount to anything at all, yet they presume I'm one of them—no different from them! Maybe that's why I feel so amused. Just now glanced around. Safe to say not one person in the place has given me a second glance. Certainly am amused. If only they knew! I admit that right now I haven't been or done anything special, have got a job maybe not much different from other people here, but of course that's not the point. I'm going to BE somebody one of these days, which means I already AM somebody. Not one of the sweepings of San Francisco, not Earl Summerfield! Look around! Old old women with swollen ankles and battered hats. Toughs with pimples, sideburns, leather boots, rings of keys hooked to their belts—guess they ride motorcycles. They're Nothing. Not one of them, not a single one is going to be anything else. Get old, paunchy, still try to act tough. Street full of them. And the old gray men turning pages of newspaper they probably picked out of a trash can. See them studying the paper like they expect to come across a notice announcing they've been elected to board of directors of Bank of America. Yes, this is where they live, places like this, shabby hotels around the corner, all-night hotdog stands, etc. I feel like getting down on my knees to pray & thank God I'm just a spectator.

Yes indeed Earl Summerfield, you're feeling all right today. That's a welcome change. So many days I feel discouraged, resentful. Maybe I pity myself, I shouldn't. Have good health and a job, can't expect Everything. I suppose one reason I get angry over trifles is that I'm counting on that supervisor's job more than I realized. I should get it. I deserve it, although I'm not the first person whose abilities have been neglected. However, I am optimistic. Yes, I am!

Excellent. Return to the apartment, see if B's at home. Have an honest talk with her. So much has gone wrong between us, but I do love her. Also, I believe she still loves me. She's right, I'm the one at fault. I'll try to improve.

FEBRUARY 11

Realize now that we never loved each other. Remembering what she said to me just one minute ago makes me want to cut a piece out of her belly. She doesn't care if I live or die, in fact she'd rather I was dead. She as much as said so. She's never loved anybody. But of course I haven't either. I'm sorry about that, truly am. I'd like to know what it means to be in love with—oh, with Anything. Just about Anything on earth, but my opinion is that love eludes certain people.

FEBRUARY 12

Bureau closed on account of Lincoln's birthday. Began raining at noon & hasn't let up. I'm sorry the office was closed, don't know how to occupy myself during the day. Look forward to tomorrow. Fensdeicke stopped at my window just before closing yesterday to say she's been tabulating the interviews and found that during the past 6 months I've made just 11 minor errors, couple of serious ones, plus the usual omissions. Not bad. She had to pretend those 2 were serious but we both understood. It was decent of her to tell me. She wasn't obliged to. She stopped by to hand along a compliment. That was nice of her. She's all right. Remarked that she feels my attitude is good, and both she and Mr. Foxx are of the opinion I stand a very good chance of promotion within the year! Well, that made me grin. Class II would mean more money—to say nothing of

Prestige. Class II, Earl Summerfield. I like the sound of that. And of course one thing leads to another. Yes, that would be a major step.

FEBRUARY 13

I'm getting fat. One hundred and sixty pounds and I'm embarrassed to set the figure down. Belt has felt tight recently, but deluded myself into thinking it was some sort of temporary indigestion. Felt inflated but thought it was air. Well, apparently not. Cut out the pie and potatoes. Face has been looking fuller & and I noticed that, too, but was unwilling to admit the truth. Working where I do doesn't help matters. Perched on that stool I can practically feel my rear expanding. I must look like a duck. No wonder, day after day, eight hours motionless as a blob of lard. Then come home to a wretched Instant Supper full of carbohydrates because she doesn't have time—she claims. Papers to grade, et cetera. For all I know she could be composing love poems to Spach. Hypocrisy. She's more interested in becoming Vice Principal than in me. I suppose she'll get the appointment—usually gets what she wants. I should say Always. I like being on top, she says. Indeed! But she's never asked what I enjoy. Oh, I could think back—yes, there used to be times, but no longer. Much too busy now. If I ask for anything special she stares at me as though I was a spoiled child. "Earl what is the matter with you?" Sorry, I say, sorry. I wonder just how many times I've spoken that word. Thousands. I'm always apologizing, if not to Bianca to somebody else. Fensdeicke. Others. That lady I accidentally bumped into yesterday. Thought she was going to Do something about it—suspicion written all over her face. Kept on apologizing. Finally she let me go. Doesn't make sense. I should have kicked her and then run for my life.

38

FEBRUARY 14

Being Valentine's Day decided to give myself a taste of luxury. Waited till Bianca was asleep before preparing things—bath salts, candlelight, etc. In certain ways I suppose I'm more like a woman than a man, but that's usually true of exceptional men although I can't imagine why. Matter of sensitivity. Certainly I'm aware of more than say Vladimir or McAuliffe. Wonder if I could be an undiscovered genius. Musician or some such. Heard of a bakery worker who picked up a violin when he was about 40 years old and realized for the first time that he'd been wasting his life. By then it was too late for him. Maybe I have some talent like that. Don't know what it is. I could become a scientist or important figure in the world of business or—what? What? What? If only I could find out! After 30 years of civil service when it's too late, maybe then I'll know. Have a feeling I'm on earth for a purpose. Don't want to waste myself. I know I'm exceptional, sure of it, just that so far nobody's given me the chance. Trapped in the Bureau, day after day, don't know how it all got started & it seems harder and harder to get out. Bianca doesn't help me, suppose she assumes I couldn't do anything else. Assumes I'm useless. Well, anyway, went to sleep in the bathtub, woke with her hammering at the door & calling me names. Water was cool so I suppose I slept quite a while. Don't know what I should have done. Should have told her off somehow instead of dabbling my fingers and waiting for it to blow over. One of my weaknesses, too passive. I always let things happen to me, as though I don't really have a personality of my own. Maybe I'm just afraid to defend myself. Don't know for sure. Probably a good idea to have things out with her—let her know I'm not what she thinks I am. Oh, I could agree with her on certain points, admit I'm far from perfect, then point out that neither is she! No argument there & that would give us both a chance to discuss the situation. Ideas fester in silence, things get poisoned. Seems that we're usually drifting into ugly positions without meaning it. Last Saturday those two—a thousand times since then I've seen that one with her fat legs spread beneath the table. Waving her knees while she sucked on a pencil. Frowning, then giggling as if she didn't know! Glancing at me. Pulling at her skirt. Nobody's going to tell me it wasn't on purpose, she knew exactly what she was doing. Think how satisfying it would be to make her suffer. Slice into those pudgy warm thighs with a razor. Yes, then tell Bianca to put the blame where it belongs! Tell B to make them act decently. But of course she's always enjoyed scolding me, it's happened often enough. As a matter of fact B might have been in on that because she didn't say a word when that little slut opened up, then when I was fool enough to get closer she was after me green with rage—except it wasn't any sort of rage, it was Excitement. My lioness.

FEBRUARY 15

News report tonight says some divorcee in San Rafael woke up early this morning and saw a man standing beside her bed with a stocking mask over his face. According to the newscaster she got away. I doubt it. Have a feeling she was tied up with a sheet—almost as though I dreamed it. Trussed like a dainty white animal, tied into a sack so tight she could only move her toes, the Parts hanging out of the mouth—those hairy purple lips. Packed stiff as a sausage. Probably gagged & blindfolded so she looked like a mummy and couldn't struggle. Flashlight, gloves, etc.

Groans, whispers. Probably he used a knife. Makes me think of savages drawing pictures on walls of their cave showing animals with spears sticking out all over them, blood streaming down their sides. That's how it was, she didn't get away. Doubt if she wanted to get away. No proof that she struggled. After all, they get accustomed to being tied up, examined. Enjoying every minute of it. I know what they are. I'm tempted to tell Bianca, ask what she thinks. For a joke might ask how she'd like it if I crawled through a window some night after she's gone to sleep. I could tie her to the bed. Then carve away! Yes, see how she likes it. Or shove in a broomstick—a bird on a spit! That would serve her right for what she's done to me. Sits at her dressing table polishing her fingernails and realize I'm married to a hag with spots on her hands. Looks older than she is, maybe that's the reason she takes it out on me. Those creases in her neck, hair getting stringy, teeth yellow from smoking & her eyes puffy. She looks at least forty years old and every day she's cutting me into little parts. Another 6 months & there won't be much left.

FEBRUARY 16

Saturday. Execution scheduled for Monday has been postponed. Legal squabbling. However, the chamber's scrubbed and inspected, the metalware polished every week whether we're having a sacrifice or not. I'd like to visit the place, chat with the men on Death Row. It sounds extremely interesting. McA says they're allowed out of their cells two hours a day and are permitted to walk up and down the corridor and play table tennis, but are not permitted to see outside. No matter how long they stay there they don't once see the water of the bay or the countryside—not from the moment they're carted through the gate until they're carted out again to be buried. Thinking about it puts me in a strange mood.

And so to bed.

FEBRUARY 17

Sunday. Bianca tutoring. Decided that I couldn't put up with it. Went out, slammed the door, spent today riding around the city on one bus after another while attempting to organize my thoughts, gain control of myself. Bus to the beach was crowded, found myself pressing against a girl in beret and a red coat. She looked at me over her shoulder, I pretended not to notice. I must have looked as bland as a dish of pudding. Got off when she got off, followed, glared at her to see what effect it would have. She heard my steps I think but didn't once glance back, walking faster and faster into the fog. Too bad it wasn't night. Wanted to hit her on the back of the neck with something sharp. Amused me to watch her scurrying along clikety-clik. Pretended I didn't exist, even so there wasn't a doubt in my mind about her being afraid. Put my hand in my pocket, squeezing away, and she knew what I was doing. If it wasn't what she wanted why had she darkened her eyes with cosmetics? Why? Lips painted, shaved legs. I'll never believe they aren't inviting us to do whatever we want to do. Shouted something at her. Remember being surprised at that because I wasn't thinking about saying anything to her, wasn't even planning to get close to her—then all at once the shout. She started running and right then I got wet and just stood there for several minutes looking around. Don't know what happened to her, where she disappeared to. Don't know why I stood there. Gazing around like a dog with an egg in its teeth, then strolled off. Most of all I can't understand why I shouted. Had no intention of doing that. The more I think about it the more puzzled I am. As though somebody inside of me is actually the one who's giving orders. Hmm! Don't like this idea because I've always been proud of my self-control. Maybe that, too, is an illusion. If so, what's left? If I can't account for myself I'm nothing.

FEBRUARY 18

McAuliffe again asked to borrow money. Last time he asked I refused and felt guilty ever since, so this time lent it to him. $20—he swears he'll pay it back next week. I hope so. Yes, I know he will.

Aside from that an uneventful day. Sun came out for a while—somebody said. I wouldn't know. Blinds lowered as always. I never have understood the reason. If the Bureau doesn't want us to know what's going on outside why did they build those enormous windows? I ought to ask but Fensdeicke wouldn't know either. It's simply the policy, she'd say, and think it was odd of me to ask. No sense risking criticism. Blinds down permanently and there we are—ninety of us illuminated by those fluorescent tubes like so many insects. I think it would be more cheerful working inside a casket. If a laborer comes through the door dripping and leaves a puddle on the linoleum I can make a guess about the weather, otherwise no telling. Overcast when I walked into that mausoleum this A.M. and overcast when I was released at 5. If the sun came out today I'd have to take somebody's word for it.

What else? Photograph in the paper of a woman in New York or someplace back there being carried out of a burning hotel. She was unconscious, at least it looked that way, her head flung back. Nightgown had blown apart & showed precious little triangle of flesh as white as cheese. Thinking about it makes me nervous, I ought to stop. If not I know what I'll do. Reminds me of McA talking about that hotel chambermaid who was held prisoner for several weeks and tortured. He claims her little Passageway was stuffed full of lighted cigarettes, but of course he may have invented the story just to see how I reacted. In either case I was careful not to reveal my thoughts.

Otherwise? The usual. Deadly tedium. That's just how I feel. Sluggish. Depressed. Bored. I don't know what to do. Try to comprehend what goes on around me day and night but it's hopeless. I'm shoved to the Left, dragged to the Right. How long has it been since anybody on earth asked for my opinion about anything? What difference does it make what I believe or what I want? Does anybody listen? Nobody even sees me.

FEBRUARY 19

Washington's Birthday next Friday, something to be grateful for. B's school and the office both close. I could ask if she'd like to see the parade, or go to Aquatic Park for the program. Possibly both, although there'll be a crowd. We'll have to go early to get a seat in the grandstand. It's worth a try.

Enough for tonight. I'm worn out. Might be wise to conceal this. She doesn't care what I do, just the same I think she's curious and might come in here while I'm away, pry around. All right, Earl, think of a secret place.

FEBRUARY 20

According to news on TV we've developed a missile they say is capable of carrying more Death & Destruction than ever before in all human history. Looks like pretty soon we're going to be able to split the world in half. Might be a good idea. Why not? Why build these things if we don't use them? Use them!—That's how I feel. Nothing but hate in the world. Take today. Some old woman praying in front of a candle at All Hallows when a Mexican hopped out from behind a statue of the Virgin, dragged her by the hair up the steps to the altar, tore off her clothes and was kicking her in the face when a priest appeared. Apparently no surprise to parishioners—they say it happens so often they usually go there to pray in groups. Too dangerous alone. Plenty of other examples, in fact so many I forget them in an hour.

So ends a typical Wednesday.

FEBRUARY 21

Sick of those greedy laborers outside the door every morning waiting for us to open—I can read their thoughts by the expression in their eyes—wondering what sort of mood Mr. Summerfield is in. Wondering if they'd be smart to come back later in the day when I won't ask so many questions, just let them go ahead and collect the money. I know everything that goes through their empty heads. Wondering if maybe it would be smart to try a different window—try Mr. Clegg or Mr. McAuliffe or Mr. Rostov. They think they're fooling me. I could give them some information on that account, but on the other hand why should I care if they're trying to cheat the State?—so is everybody else. Evading taxes, swindling, etc. There isn't much decency left in the world. Not very much. In my opinion whatever there was went up in a column of smoke above Hiroshima. We set the past on fire. Quite a performance all right. I more or less remember it. Ashes everywhere, still sifting down. Ideals smirched, avarice, self-righteousness—

45

the Holy Sepulcher just one more milestone on the road to some cloudy Fulfillment. Fulfillment of what! Cheating, lying, riots, war, wax, oil, iron, sulfur, wine, papyrus & eternal slavery. Jesus Christ in Heaven.

I'm tired, sick at heart. Not much hope. Maybe suicide's not wrong.

FEBRUARY 22

Washington's Birthday. Bianca didn't want to go, claimed she had to talk with Spach about organizing a teachers' association of some sort. It was just one more excuse to avoid going anywhere with me, I wasn't taken in by it but I really don't care. Am used to being alone. Let her have tea and cookies with Spach, do as she pleases, get down on her knees in front of him if she cares to, it means nothing to me! Someday she'll be damned for what she does. We pay for what we do in this world. Sooner or later the wheel comes full circle for us all.

Besides, it's a good thing she didn't go because she would have gotten bored in 5 minutes and insisted on leaving. Folk dancers, mandolin player, magician, Hollywood actors giving declarations of faith in America, only place on earth where there's any freedom, etc. Sweetness and more sweetness. Crap! Make-believe. Also a long dull speech about constitutional guarantees and so forth by our ex-Governor. People in the grandstand were coughing, eating peanuts, yawning but then of course applauding when he was finished. I felt like vomiting on the platform, let them see what their beautiful nation really stands for. They ought to have a good look at America. No doubt it looks very nice from a distance, just be sure you don't get too close. Then you find out. Bigotry, fraud, immorality—no use cataloguing it! In short, the whole business soured my stomach right from the beginning. Five thousand people getting to their feet to sing the national anthem and then recite the Pledge of Allegiance but I know what was in their hearts and in their minds. I know what they do every day and every night. I wonder if I was the only one who mouthed the words but didn't utter a sound. No, probably there were others. Must be a few other people who realize how decayed this country is. Then that bitch in the bathing suit climbed up on the stage wearing a cardboard crown & carrying a scepter, went parading back and forth to show off her tits. No shame. No modesty. Program said she was a dramatics student at University of California—Mara St. Johns. She looked to me like one of those professional sluts from Hollywood. If she isn't the symbol of American rottenness, what is? Program said she was active in the Presbyterian church! There's hypocrisy for you Earl, but some day the wheel is going to come full circle for her too—for her and all the others like her. For the dirty things they do. Pretending to be what they're not. In fact the longer I think about it the more it seems to me this whole nation is going to lie in ashes and lumps of pitch just as the Bible predicted. Was it there? Mmm—well, wherever. Doesn't matter, message is the same. Nation that rules the earth shall go astray, future will see it deserted. Evil to increase a thousandfold. The sun shall shine by night and the moon by day! Blood come trickling out of wood. Stones make a roaring noise like the wind. People are going to be troubled and courses change. Sea will cast out its fish, birds fly off separately and One shall come to reign over us for whom those on Earth do not hope—but they will recognize his voice. Yes, indeed they will! And if that's so who's going to be surprised? After what we've seen the last few years?

Well, maybe I ought to ask Bianca. She's always got an opinion no matter what the subject is. Too bad she didn't want to attend the show, then I could explain my theory,

47

find out what she thinks of it. Wish she'd wanted to go with me. Been so long since—feel so lonely. Wish we could have what we used to have. Three or four years ago we'd go out dancing but now she doesn't ever come near me if she can avoid it.

What would happen if I apologized and tried to get in bed?

FEBRUARY 23

The other day I asked V if he thought there was such a thing as Love. Said there isn't. Claimed it was an invention of poets, some lice-covered troubadours in southern France during the Middle Ages & ever since then we've believed it actually exists. I don't know, don't know what to think, what to believe. So confused. B hates me.

FEBRUARY 24

Sunday. She's in Oakland visiting her sister & I've spent half the day marching around and around like a mechanical soldier with a key in my back. Nothing to eat since breakfast, then not much. Hungry but can't make myself stop long enough to fix a meal. The weather's nice & I guess everybody else is out enjoying the afternoon in Sausalito or Golden Gate Park. I'd give anything to be as average as that. Knowing you're superior is a curse. Also, not having the opportunity to make use of my abilities makes it difficult to keep sense of proportion.

Around & around! Have drawn the shades so at least it's dark. Feeling a little better, yet can't decide what troubles me. Admit I'm still exasperated by the celebration, pageant, whatever it was. Should have reached up, grabbed one of her ankles and jerked her down off the stage. She was close enough, just above me. Could have reached up and pushed my finger right into that hairy mound. She knew it— glanced down at me. In fact that's probably what she wanted me to do. Corruption. Filth. The whore of Washington's Birthday. I'm not good enough for you, is that it? You glance down at me and walk away smiling. Well, I'm not going to forget you! Saintly nun. Ermine cloak and a pasteboard crown—Screw! I'd fix you if I had a chance, don't think I wouldn't. I'd give you a crown to wear. A jeweled prick. It's what you deserve. It's what you want, too, if I'm much of a judge.

B still isn't back from Oakland, guess she might stay overnight. I wish she'd come home.

FEBRUARY 25

After work paid a visit to All Hallows Church, can't say quite why except that it's been on my mind since the Mexican attacked that old woman praying. No accident. He went there to show everybody something—yes, but what? What? What? Church was smaller than I expected, only about half visible through some ragged windblown palms on Dolores Street. Paint flaking off the rail, steps creaked. Could hardly pull the door open. Nobody inside. Candles burning in front of some statues. Priest came walking down the aisle toward me, his face black with suspicion until he saw that I was Respectable. Until he noticed I was dressed in a business suit, then he changed right away. Shook hands, etc. Chatted with him for a while, acted sympathetic to his problem. Hoodlums ransack the poorbox, says he. Amazed, outraged, I put on my show of anger, and he points to the boxes broken open & hanging along the wall. Boys not old enough to shave, says he, with switchblade knives prying open those boxes. Clasped my hands in disbelief. Absolutely can't believe it! I exclaim. Collection envelopes stolen, says he. How awful! No respect for Anything these days. Etc. True, True & he wags his head. Tells me police cars cruise the neighborhood after every parish gathering—doing our best to protect the flock, not much use. Dreadful! I said. Dreadful! Then cleared my throat. My wife and I are thinking we'd like to move into this neighborhood & being devout I wanted to see your church. I shall pray, says he, that you and Mrs. Summerfield choose to join us. Could hardly swallow my laughter.

FEBRUARY 26

Not much change since yesterday—am in a pukey humor. Seems to me that Civilization is spinning toward the Pit. No matter where I look. Those big-shot corporation executives the other day convicted by federal Grand Jury of conspiring to violate some regulation or other—millions of dollars involved, brigades of lawyers from 5th Avenue or wherever they have those swank offices. What's the penalty? Tap on the wrist. Judge gives them "stern warning." That's about what I expected. They've got the money, the position. That judge was probably scared to death, knew if he did to them what he ought to do they'd ruin him. But let Earl Summerfield swipe an apple—oh oh! Convicted of theft, fined, put on close probation. If I took two dozen apples I'd rot in jail. Why should anybody respect the law! I used to. Yes, I remember when I did, but now I've learned how things really are. I can't be fooled any longer. Believe very little that I'm told, investigate for myself. The government lies to me and people on the street lie to me. Sometimes get the feeling I'm walking on a flimsy little bridge stretched across a canyon. Wind blowing & people shouting at me from both sides. Maybe it's easier to quit, just step over the rail. I don't know.

Could be the monotony of the office that makes me feel like this. Get away Earl! Get away before it's too late. How? Sometimes I wish I lived in the middle of Egypt. Anyplace. Would be willing to trade my soul for one hour of hot sunlight instead of this rain. February rain. Rain.

Get away. How? I keep asking. Another month's almost gone & what have I got to show for it? How many more? I realize I'm much too intelligent for my job, that's one thing that depresses me. Forced to spend every day talking to laborers so stupid that one of these days think I might just give up the use of language and resort to signs. Why doesn't the Bureau recognize my ability? Why can't Mrs. Fensdeicke grasp the fact that I should be assigned to important work? It's possible she does know and is worried that I'll get her job, or even that Mr. Foxx may promote me to some position where she'll have to take orders from me. Mr. Summerfield, pardon me, but we need your initials on this. Mr. Summerfield, excuse us, but would you give us your opinion about this case? Then I could have an office of my own, wouldn't be perched on that stool with my rump exposed. Sitting there I feel like a miserable fool, people smiling at me behind my back.

FEBRUARY 27

Wednesday. There's s-silver, pl-pl-platinum and gold in the sea! says Magnus. Yes, it's there, no doubt, in the sand along the coast and in the mouths of rivers, carried down from the Mother Lode. And offshore are traces of copper, manganese, iron, cobalt, all brought up by currents from the ocean bottom. Won't be long until miners go to work thousands of feet below the surface on the bedrock of the Pacific. Submerged capsules will be traveling across the shelf like lobsters, or hanging in mid-ocean undisturbed by the turmoil of the upper world. True enough, nobody with any sense would doubt that prediction—not any more, not after what's happened these past few years. But how is Magnus going to profit by all this? That's what I can't understand. He seems to think he's going to benefit, whereas the truth is he won't, neither of us will. The profits of the future will go where the profits of the past have gone—into the pockets of the admirals, the generals, the waxy old men slumped in the backs of limousines. Not a penny for Magnus, not a penny for Earl. Why doesn't he realize that's how it is? Says he's going to Arizona on his vacation to hunt for gemstones in the desert. Somebody down there discovered a jade boulder weighing a thousand pounds. Maybe. Maybe not. Suppose it's true, will Magnus find another one? He won't find a thing, no more than I would. Why? Because we don't live at the right address. Life's just that simple. Poor Magnus is going to spend his two weeks in Arizona sifting pebbles through a sieve. Well, he's as likely to make his fortune as I am—perhaps I should stop being such a realist and join him. Shut my eyes, stuff rubber plugs in my ears. Nod & bow & smile.

FEBRUARY 28

Have been thinking that perhaps I grip myself too tightly. I squeeze myself dry, that could be the trouble. I'm too careful, too discreet. Pick a path through life avoiding—avoiding what? Absolutely everything, in fact. I can't Allow anything to happen, I've got to plan it. I want it to happen on schedule. Caught up with me today—turned my face to the ceiling and let loose a howl. Nobody heard. What if tomorrow I opened my mouth and did it? At least I'd be noticed. That could be what I need. I keep waiting, waiting, avoiding trouble, assuming that before much longer I'll be recognized. How soon? I'm afraid to attract attention to myself but at the same time I hate this anonymity. Christ. Oh Jesus Christ! If only I knew what would become of me.

MARCH 1

This month began on a delightful note. Going to work thought I'd act polite, held open the door for a group of women. Not one of them mentioned it, not one bothered to look at me. I might just as well be a pile of shit on the sidewalk.

MARCH 2

Saturday. Seagulls drifting overhead. Drizzling rain starts, then quits. Accident at the corner, somebody was killed I think but didn't go down to investigate because didn't want to put on a raincoat etc. Bianca went to Oakland again, sister's pregnant. Ho hum twiddle dum.

Can't say what became of this Saturday, like so many others, gone before I knew it. Maybe because I didn't do anything. Absolutely nothing. Never accomplish anything on weekends, don't even get any exercise. Haven't played a game of golf or had a swim or even a horseback ride in years. Sit around making plans that don't work out. Hours today imagining what I'd like to do to that beauty queen if I saw her again. First of all I'd leave some fat red blisters where she'd feel them.

Just now looked in the telephone book. Didn't expect to find her name but there it was—Mara St. Johns. Simple as that! Lives on Vallejo near Steiner. Also a Mrs. Arthur St. Johns at the same address but a different telephone. Must be one of those fancy apartment buildings with a doorman. Means they've got money. Hmm. Thinking back, yes, the sort that's got everything. Looks, money, expensive education, all the rest of it. I've seen plenty of them like that—conceited bitches that won't even speak to you. Don't know you're alive. You're not good enough. Snotty, selfish—oh yes I know them. Probably got one of those foreign sports cars and goes racing across the bridge every morning to the campus. That's the type. So superior! What I wouldn't do if—ha ha! If. If.

Certain people were born lucky. I wasn't.

MARCH 3

Weather changed overnight, by this afternoon the streets were dry and it felt more like May or June. Took the bus to Aquatic Park, loitered in the grandstand, removed my shirt—discovered I'm white as a corpse. Inside too much, that's natural but I don't like it. Feeling that I'm not Existing. Feel as though I'm made of wax. Imitation. I feed on the newspapers, TV. Look in the mirror & get back a reflection but not of myself. Can't go by a window without peeking in hoping—hoping for what? Some expression of life, I guess. Useless & delusory. Think of myself in front of cameras. Dreams of getting Away—making myself over. I wonder what people think when they look at me, if they're curious as to who I am. Oh probably not. Why should they be? Who's Earl Summerfield? Nobody. Well, I'm not alone. At least I have the satisfaction of knowing that the people around me aren't any more important than I am. Those convicts scheduled to be executed this week—Friday? Two in the morning, two after lunch. They're going to be gassed the same way society disposes of stray dogs, only difference I suppose is that they'll be put on display. Animals at the market. What's that got to do with me? Nothing. Wonder how they're feeling right now. Would like to get in touch with them—that would be very interesting.

3 A.M. Still awake. Little while ago rummaged about in the kitchen and found the newspaper. Description of gas chamber, says it'll smell like almond blossoms and their faces will flush deep red, after which it's Oblivion. Booker Jackson, 28, foundry worker, held up a grocery store in Los Angeles & shot a customer. Ford Lesso, 21, no trade, killed a deputy sheriff who tried to arrest him for speeding. Purvis Sandifer, 36, merchant seaman, raped 85-year-old woman. Raymond Welch, 42, gas-station attendant, robbed and shot a bank messenger. Unimportant men every one. That's how it is. Four men tumbling into the grave because they've been miserable and small. Not one of them had the faculty of impressing his personality on the world. That's a lesson worth remembering.

MARCH 4

Most of today thinking about that woman sunbathing yesterday in the park. I should have spoken to her, but was too timid, as always. I glare at them, hoping they'll be attracted to me, but they turn away & I don't blame them. I'm not the sort to attract anybody, man or woman. I guess little Magnus must be the only person on earth who's beneath me. I look up to everybody else. Despise McAuliffe, yet I respect and envy him. Clegg I don't like, want nothing to do with him, but admit I'm intimidated. What's become of the friends I used to have? Floated out of sight one after

56

the other. Couples don't visit us any more either, which isn't surprising. B's critical of everybody and I've never been good at entertaining. Have never understood how to put people at ease. If only I felt confident enough to approach somebody. That woman yesterday—just to talk with her, just that would have been enough, would have made me feel more like a man. I could have smiled, commented about the weather & sailboats on the bay instead of sitting on the rail like a bird whistling and staring at her. Well, maybe it's best I didn't speak—she'd have ignored me. She's like all the others, suspicious, conceited tramp. I hope she gets what's coming to her, that's all I hope!

MARCH 5

Body of a music student discovered this A.M. on the steps of City College, sweater & underclothing pulled up like a mask across her face. Diane somebody, seventeen years old. Odd there's nothing in the paper about it, I'm positive I heard it on the radio just as I was waking up. Bianca must have heard, however it wouldn't be wise to ask. She'd wonder why I was inquiring. Still, that's odd. I did hear a voice. The details are clear, almost as though I'd seen a photograph. Her head was propped up against the steps, eyes open, blood on her lips where she'd first been struck, sheets of music scattered about, a pack of dogs attracted by the peculiar scent nosing between her thighs. Well, no matter if I heard it or not, the voice of God is everywhere.

What else today? Snowstorm in the Sierras. How I'd love to be there! I should learn to ski, visit the mountains every weekend, lots of people do. No reason I couldn't, except the expense. And the fact that Bianca would say it was foolish. She wouldn't want to go & consequently would make certain that I felt like an imbecile for suggesting it. Takes several hours to get there so you'd have Saturday afternoon, would need to start back about Sunday noon. I'll give it some thought.

Otherwise not much. I don't understand why McAuliffe doesn't return the money he borrowed, remember him saying he would by the end of last week at the latest. If he doesn't give it to me by this Friday I'll mention it. I'm sure he means to pay me back, probably just slipped his mind.

MARCH 6

Quite an agreeable surprise as I was leaving the office! Fensdeicke stopped me to say I've been late to work fewer times than anybody else in the department. What she was actually saying was that she's been keeping an eye on me & that means I'm due for the new supervisory position. Couldn't be another reason for going out of her way to compliment me. Of course she only makes the recommendations so she couldn't flatly tell me I'm on the way up, but that's what it must mean. Well, Earl, at last! I'd just about lost hope. How much difference a little bit of news can make. Yesterday I was depressed, nervous, walking back & forth washing my hands in the air, running my fingers through my hair, pinching my lip, feverish, full of ugly thoughts, but now I'm practically elated. Things are going to be all right, I guess it's just putting in so much time at the Bureau and being ignored for so long—I'm too quick to condemn people. The Bureau's a large, complex affair and there must be many employees who deserve promotion even more than I do. Do I give them much of a thought? No, always thinking about myself, as though I was the only person in the world. I ought to get over that. Sin of Pride. What causes it? Well, knowing I'm superior to most, which is certainly true

—that's the danger. I'll try to keep a sense of proportion, make certain allowances for others not so lucky as I am.

Further thought. I realize I'm glad Clegg isn't getting that supervisor's job. I realize I was afraid he'd get it. Why? They say he's got money & only works here to have something to do. He doesn't look rich, but you can't ever tell. If so that would explain why he hates the Communists so much—scared to death they'll come marching over to take it away from him and divide it up. Would serve him right. Whether he is or not I don't need to be afraid of him much longer, won't need to tiptoe past him. Those cranky humors & so forth—he reminds me of some old man out of the last century with that white speck in his eye and those formal manners that don't mean a thing. He should have lived when Ladies were hanging frilled petticoats around piano legs, that's his sort of Decency. Well, he'd better dance a minuet after I become a supervisor. Others, too! Magnus is careful, few mistakes, but doesn't show initiative, and he's slow. I'll get more work out of him. Vladimir does his work well enough, no complaint there, except for leaving all that ridiculous socialist literature on the counter. Fensdeicke's warned him twice, both times claimed he "forgot." He's doing it deliberately and is aware it's against the rules. I'll see it doesn't happen any more, he knows he can't fool me. But as for McAuliffe, don't know how to get much more work out of him, he has so many ways to avoid doing what he's expected to do. However, that'll be a challenge. Many challenges for me, but I feel up to them. As soon as I've been promoted I'll whip some life into our department and I daresay Sacramento is soon going to be talking about "that new supervisor in San Francisco!" Oh yes, we've been hearing—etc., etc. What's his name? Well, soon enough they're going to be finding out! Yes indeed! Then after a while—maybe during vacation—could catch a bus to Sacramento, drop by the central office and say I'm just there to have a look around. That way they'd get a close look at me. Next year another step up.

Grateful. Yes, I truly am! I was beginning to feel like a turtle but things will be different from now on.

MARCH 7

Occurred to me this P.M. that I'm getting fussy. Too neat. Picking at details. Arranging paper clips, reciting State regulations without being the least bit interested in what I'm saying. Monotony does it, I suppose. I've been there so long facing a blank wall. What I need is the respect of some important people, invitations to parties on Pacific Heights and Nob Hill. I'd like to belong to some of those fancy clubs where everybody's got a pedigree. Why don't I? What's keeping me from it? I'm smart and have good taste in various things, could study up in my spare time about cultural subjects. In fact I could start going to the symphony and opera and at intermission during those affairs they get together at the bar. Yes, that would be a way to get acquainted with them. Wouldn't be long before I'd be accepted. Once I've become a supervisor I could tell them what I do without feeling ashamed. All that holds me down at present is not having any money or the right opportunities. Important to change my pattern. Must not go on like this. Don't want to get trapped in fixed, rigid ways like Clegg, for instance. Year after year—because that could be a sign of danger. I've noticed how occasionally something seems to snap inside his brain, loud enough I can almost hear it. Courteous as you please, then pop!—usually when he's talking to one of the blacks. He hates them, I can sense it. He wouldn't admit it. Makes me think of a brick building ready to collapse. He's too polite, too quick to smile and show his false teeth. Plenty of people around like that, I'm not fooled by their smiles.

MARCH 8

Sandifer, Welch & Jackson executed. Lesso reprieved because of some sort of technicality. Usual last-minute flurry of telephone calls, attorney rushing around the city trying to get hold of a certain judge to obtain a writ or whatever it's called. Newscast said a traffic light was red, which delayed the attorney 30 seconds, otherwise Sandifer might have been reprieved. Of course this whole affair makes sense, it's just that I'm not able to understand it. How many years were they on Death Row? Forgotten, but then finally life or death hangs on a traffic light. You couldn't produce a play like that because the audience would walk out, it's too stupid. Anyway I'm glad they're dead.

B finally decided to let go of the evening paper. Article about the executions says Lesso got a "stay of execution" instead of a reprieve. Not sure what the difference is, anyway he's got 30 more days to play checkers while they go on squabbling about the case. I wonder if he'll be able to concentrate on checkers. I think I'd be practicing hymns. "Nearer My God to Thee." Well, that's his problem, not mine. Although as a matter of fact I haven't been feeling so cheerful myself recently. So much alone. And always this sense that I'm being Scrutinized. Every time I turn around I find somebody staring at me. Considering wearing tinted glasses, that would make me feel more secure but might cause some comment at the office. Fensdeicke marks down everything & it might go on my report. Don't want anything unfavorable, don't want anything to interfere with my promotion.

So much for this week. Two days of freedom ahead. Hope I get over my cold before long. Sneezing & coughing.

MARCH 9

Another Saturday up the chimney. Those two little whores were here again. I was careful to avoid them, didn't so much as say hello when they came in, which ought to let them know what I think of them. Stayed in here playing the radio until they were gone. Bianca refused to cook dinner so made myself a sandwich, watched TV awhile, then took a walk. Stopped at the movie arcades on Market —full of sailors, then down as far as the Embarcadero, where I stopped for coffee. Rode a jitney out Mission and then walked some more. I probably walked about fifteen miles tonight but didn't feel tired. Coming back went through alleys and back yards around Duboce, etc., looking looking looking, pausing at windows. At one place some man started after me, but pointed ahead as though I lived in the next building & hurried along before anything happened. Avoiding trouble is a matter of being quick-witted. I'm that, whatever else I'm not. Also, another place, brushed against clothes drying on a rope—odor has a strange effect, odor of clothes. I might go back.

MARCH 10

Visited the De Young museum this afternoon for lack of much else to do. Exhibit of sculpture from India. There was an admission fee so nearly passed it up but am glad I didn't. Women carved out of limestone, most of them dancing, with bells on their ankles. When the guard turned away I bent down and pressed my cheek against one of

62

the bellies. Cool and rough, a thousand years old but gave me the feeling that it still pulsed with life.

Bianca at work on a sheaf of papers when I returned & didn't ask where I'd been. My Love, are you so sure of me? In fact, she isn't because occasionally I catch her observing me—as though I was an elephant or a crocodile. What's she thinking? If I wanted to I could put myself in her place and find out, simpler than it seems. Women limited, fancies predictable. She suspects, yet doesn't know What she suspects, just that whatever it is she doesn't like it. In her way she's shrewd enough but I don't have much trouble deceiving her because I'm blessed with the power of original thought, she's not. Oh, she talks when she feels like it & talks brilliantly when there's company, yes, I'm the first to admit her brilliance, but even at her wittiest she doesn't have a thing to say.

MARCH 11

Scandal at the Bureau today—McAuliffe came to work with liquor on his breath and was sent home after first being called to Foxx's office. Fensdeicke won't say what happened but there's no doubt he got a severe warning. Was planning to ask him today how soon he'd return my loan. Thinking about it makes me angry. He's had time enough. I could use the money. Ask him tomorrow.

Otherwise nothing in particular. Police raided a massage parlor. Say they kept the place under surveillance for 2 months, counted taxicabs, clients, etc. Men swarming in and out like grasshoppers. Women, clients, police—equally filthy. There's not much decency left in the world, that's my opinion. But of course I'm too romantic, I expect too much. Should respond to life as it actually is, instead of sitting here feeding my contempt. McA for instance—he's a "deadbeat," it's what he is, might as well admit the fact. Admit I'll never get my money back. Admit it Earl. Admit you've been cheated! Cheated, cheated, cheated!

Midnight. I'm famished. I think I'll fix a snack.

MARCH 12

Headlines today. Sausalito schoolgirl disappears. Loretta Lengfeldt, age 14, last seen walking along Bridgeway a few minutes after school let out. Everybody wonders where she can be. Not a trace. Parents think she might have gone to visit grandmother and gotten lost. That makes me smile.

MARCH 13

No word of Loretta but police have several clues. Found her books in a ditch. Also, motorists now report seeing a young girl struggling with a man but they assumed it was a father punishing his daughter, so nobody stopped— what they're saying is that they didn't want to get Involved. So police bulletins go out. Loretta Lengfeldt, age 14, height 5′2″, weight 105 lbs. Last seen dressed in "powder-blue" sweater, pleated white skirt, brown moccasins and white wool socks. The little peach! Where could she be? One thing's sure—she's tucked away in a very very private place. Mother and father appeal to kidnaper not to hurt their darling, promise any reward. Bravo. Bravo. What a waste of time. A few months from now somebody's going to stumble on the remains. She won't be far from the city—umm, let's think. Some wooded hillside or a leafy glen. Lying on her side with hands tied behind her and naked as a nymph strangled with her own brassiere—that would be my guess.

Probably sliced up like a piece of pork. Got what she deserved for nibbling on a chocolate doughnut and showing her fat little buttocks to everybody on the street. Probably when they find the body they'll see teethmarks on those tender boobies, maybe a nipple missing, or an earlobe chewed off. She'd taste like an apple. Then of course everybody is going to be amazed and outraged. Citizens Councils blah blah blah! If she's out in the woods I suppose they'll send a troop of Boy Scouts to look in the caves as though they expect to find some fiend muttering & growling over a campfire. More I think about it the more disgusted I get. Why are they always so surprised! What do they expect! Those two little bitches Robin and Twinka coming in here acting the same way. It just might happen to them, they're no more decent than Lengfeldt—all three of them probably earning money after school by squirming around on their ass. Don't tell me they don't deserve to be butchered! Next Saturday or Sunday whenever they're here I'll find some way to talk to them when B isn't around—let them know what happened to sweet little Lori & exactly why.

MARCH 14

Looks like I was right again. Another one today. Lewd photos of 14-year-old girl. What sluts they are! How long is it going to be until people realize the truth? Inspectors Keith and Paoli found 60 photographs, discovered she'd been doing it several afternoons a week. Going to an apartment on Gough, paid twenty dollars every time she posed. Now they've got her in Youth Guidance Center. Inspector Keith says to reporters the little tramp "seemed like a nice child." Oh yes! As "nice" as Lengfeldt. Or these two Bianca's tutoring!

Quit thinking about it. Rottenness everywhere. Look for

good news. Well, financial pages tell us business is booming. That's fine but doesn't concern me. Secretary of State meets with Russian foreign minister in Geneva, continue haggling about bombs. Would shoot both of them if I had a chance. Hmm. What else? Vallejo hotel burned down, eight guests roasted to a crisp. They must have looked like sausages. Tomorrow that's what everybody will be discussing. How dreadful, etc. Explosions, floods, murders, fires, maybe a kitten trapped in a well. That's what the public wants to discuss. Everything of that sort has great effect on individuals of slight moral development.

Yes, I do feel I'm growing. Exfoliating—that's the word. One of B's favorites. Old flakes & scales drop off, fresh buds emerge, eyes open so that we perceive the world anew.

MARCH 15

Further thoughts about that fire. Purification. Why were those eight selected? Coincidence? Perhaps, I doubt it. I have my suspicions. There's not as much coincidence as people think. Anyway, have cut out the article & pictures to keep. Will continue to search for the hidden pattern of events. There's a divine Order all right, nobody's going to convince me different. It's difficult to recognize only because Man is so unintelligent. We can't grasp the unity that exists, all we see are the details of it. Animals in circular pen plodding around & around expecting finally to come to the end, but of course it's impossible. Animals are not intelligent enough to grasp the idea of the Circle. So it is with us in regard to whatever's enclosing us. Does our Salvation lie in awareness of our limitation? I can't say, but it's certainly worth thinking about.

MARCH 16

Divine Punishment? Who can be sure? Isaiah speaks of the man especially singled out by God but whom God keeps in obscurity like an arrow in the quiver. Certain times I'd like to be the appointed one, yes—controlling others, orders unquestioned, yes. Obedience. Power of Pharaoh announcing the Law. I think it's going to come to pass. Judging from what I read and hear about day after day we ought to be prepared. Slashing, strangling, two murders in the city this week. People talk about it, oh yes everybody's got Something to say & all pretend to be disturbed, but actually nobody really cares, just as long as it happens to somebody else. I don't think we get close to each other during our entire lives. We're like mountain peaks standing alone in the ocean, joined deep below the surface.

I expect it must be close to midnight, neglected to wind the clock. However, I think I'll stay up all night. Right now I feel like singing or shouting and my head's as full of light as a shower of meteors.

MARCH 17

As usual brooding over the past. Yesterday combing my hair for such a long long time—trying to put every single hair in place. Seemed logical yesterday, but now I'm wondering why. Why was it important? I'm neat enough, who cares how my hair is combed? Who'd notice? Should I stop somebody on the street and ask? They'd just smile & stroll off—pfft! Then today, suddenly discovered myself being so dignified. Stalking around, frowning at nothing. I've been doing that too often, am positive people have noticed. I suppose they think I'm being presumptuous, although of course they couldn't be aware that I'm on the verge of promotion. But I shouldn't act superior, retain humility. Behave with natural dignity. If that's presumption—very well, I'll be presumptuous! I'm Earl Summerfield!

MARCH 18

Lost control tonight. It was her fault, even so I was impetuous & blame myself. Or is it true we're responsible for our actions? Can't decide. Sometimes it seems that we're merely Constructions made out of yarn, paper & wood with threads rising from our toes and fingertips. We pretend to talk and act as though we were alive when actually we don't have any choice in the matter. Some secret power directs us. Tonight all of a sudden I stood up at the table and without a single word of explanation slapped B across the mouth. She'd been talking while I was trying to think, that's why she was punished. However I was only the instrument —decision to punish her wasn't made by me because I don't recall drawing back my arm—it moved by itself exactly as though pulled by a string. I was helpless to prevent it, could only watch. Knew I was going to hit her, after which she'd be forced to give back everything she'd stolen from me— convinced of this, also that as soon as I hit her she would stop acting so positive, stop giving me orders. Earl, I want you to—Earl I'm sick and tired of—Earl Earl Earl! Well, now she knows better. If she forgets what happened tonight she's going to get another lesson. But I don't think she's going to forget, looking at me now with greater respect, realized I'm not her child or some useful pet. Quite a step forward. And the next step's going to come when I tell her she's not a woman, not really. She disguises herself as one but the fact is she's actually a man—tall and scrawny with the or-

68

gans sucked up inside. Makes me a little sick at my stomach. That black wart on the tip of her nose, if she was interested in being a woman she'd get rid of it. Oh, there are so many things! Yes, but who wants to think about them? I remember eight or nine years—eight, yes, just after we met, first time I put my arms around her but instead of flesh I could feel her ribs. Other such matters by the hundred. I don't like the way she smells. Eating toast without butter, etc. Clearer each & every day how different we are, what a mistake this marriage was. I have the soul of a poet, she's a school-teacher with a mind like a blotter. If only I had in fact Actually done it—actually slapped her as hard as I could while we were sitting at the table. In that case how would things turn out? As I imagine them?

Tiptoed down the hall, opened the bedroom door a crack. She acts asleep but recently have had a feeling she shuts her eyes whenever I'm around. Not that I care, I'm relieved that she goes to bed early and leaves the night to me. Gives me a chance to develop my personality. I feel stronger at night, more confident, similar to the feeling animals must have. Emanations of the daily world are gone. Yes, I become more meaningful at night, my brain alert & flickering electrically with bright perceptions.

MARCH 19

Listening to Bianca coughing and sneezing. She never gets really sick, but a stream of small ailments to make sure I don't come near her. Think she's working on a speech she's going to deliver to a political group. She's become quite the Republican, one activity then another. As for me, she doesn't have time.

69

MARCH 20

Wednesday. Item in today's Chronicle amused me. Police officer H. H. Nyborg arrested for making obscene telephone calls. He's admitted telephoning but denies his calls were indecent, claims he was asking the lady to cook his supper. Seems he met her when her apartment was burglarized & he was sent to investigate. Have always thought police no better than the rest of us, and this confirms it, worse because they march around in uniforms as if they never did anything wrong. Screw the police. Name anybody who'd shed a tear if all of them were shoved into a pit of quicklime.

MARCH 21

Another picture of Lori Lengfeldt in the paper tonight, clipped it for the scrapbook. She makes a sweet addition to my gallery. Am tempted to send her parents a note. Dr. & Mrs. Lengfeldt: I won't reveal my identity but I noticed your charming daughter strutting around the schoolyard like a plump little hen. Now that she's been carried away and gobbled up by the wicked fox who's responsible?

Tum te te tum—wonder how much Bianca suspects. If anything. Hard to guess. Well, I won't underestimate her, not with that faculty they have for sensing the patterns of life. Suppose it's been necessary for survival, they're such defenseless animals. Well, in any case I'll be cautious, keep things hidden. No wish to be discovered.

To bed, to bed.

MARCH 22

Amusing idea while shaving—I resemble Pinocchio! All at once caught sight of my pointed nose poking through the lather and there he was!—no doubt about it. Pinocchio Summerfield. Pouting red lips. Sometimes I look like a nasty-tempered schoolgirl. But then my hairline's receding—never quite realized that I possessed such a bulging forehead. The mark of the intellectual. I've heard that Emerson had a forehead like mine. Ears must be my weakest feature—those wings have always embarrassed me. Different style of haircut might help. Sideburns? No no—ridiculous, dislike attracting attention to myself. Ought to resign myself to my appearance. My teeth aren't bad, I should smile more often. Eyebrows rather silky & faint, not dark enough to impress people—in certain lights I just don't seem to have any eyebrows. I think that's odd, considering my dark hair and beard. Well, we are as we are. Lackaday. Somehow I look right in character when my face is covered with lather. Quite an amusing little fellow Pinocchio.

Yes, on the whole I'm in better spirits tonight. Have felt depressed, irritable, cynical most of the week, some sort of moral indigestion brought on by the daily horror of the news. One can't help despising people. However, I tend to forget about the decent ones and all the splendid achievements taking place. Life's not so bad Earl, everything's going to work out all right. Often think I should have become an artist—it's a matter of some technique, and I'm a bit late for that, otherwise it's purely sensibility. I could have been —let's see. Gold. Precious gems. I'd like to work with those, create fanciful decorations as they used to do in the Renaissance. Have always loved to work with my hands, now I handle nothing but sheafs of paper. Dry and unsatisfactory,

I'm too passionate to work with sheets of paper. A shame I didn't realize this soon enough because I might have become another Benvenuto Cellini, famous halfway around the world. They say he lived a violent passionate life, was subject to awful moods, got enraged by trifles. We're much alike. I'd like to have gone along with him swaggering down the middle of a street, people bowing & backing out of your path. Audiences with kings, popes, yes, and those rich commissions. Great men of the past didn't put up with insults, they knew how to get what they wanted. But then of course in those days they were allowed to wear a sword. What a difference that would make. With a long sword dangling from your belt people would be forced to respect you.

So much for dreams. I guess there were men like me wearing swords as long & sharp as any, still nobody was deceived. Puffed up and strutting like pigeons through the alleys of Venice, scared to death somebody was going to laugh.

Well, in any event, goodnight Pinocchio, or Summerfield, or whoever you think you are.

MARCH 23

Nasty situation. Those two gum-chewing sluts leaning over their books—watched them from the bedroom, Bianca got wind of it—don't know how. Marched into the bedroom stiff with rage and ordered me in an absolutely vicious whisper to get out of the apartment & not dare come back until after 4 o'clock. Pretended not to hear, merely put on my jacket and announced I was going for a stroll. The little bitches stared at me, one of them kicked the other under the table. Went out and walked around the block several times, caught a Geary bus & calmly cut a hole in the back seat—only satisfaction I got all day. Would like to slice up two schoolgirl bellies. Remind me of fresh green melons. If they think they can make fun of me they'll regret it.

Aside from that, nothing new. Don't enjoy my Saturdays any more, it's an effort to DO things. I seem to sit on a bench and watch, might as well be middle-aged. Wind the clock at a certain hour, open each window exactly so, not an inch too high. Keep counting the coins in my pocket, wash my hands 14 times a day—wretched wretched! When she whispered at me this afternoon I could feel the tears come into my eyes. Right now she's lying awake, I can tell, waiting to accuse me again. I don't want to talk about it, just want to be left alone. Doesn't seem to me that's asking very much.

MARCH 24

They never experience the world as it truly IS— always living within themselves brooding & calculating. What do they know about the human Spirit? The universe bores them. Their only urge is toward personal satisfaction, weakening a man & sucking away the power. Jellies, mold that grows on bread, rind of rotting fruit, infection, suppuration, evil odors that drift around during the night, colorless poisons, caverns full of dead little bodies. Unclean alchemies. Yes, that tells the story of them.

MARCH 25

Interesting talk with Magnus during lunch. He says on the island of Patmos in the Aegean there's a monastery stuffed like a basket with treasure—jeweled crosses, gold chalices, Byzantine manuscripts written in gold & silver letters on red parchment, etc. I was tempted to ask what difference it makes to him. World is packed with unobtainable treasure. Floor of the ocean must be half solid gold, but the nearest that he or I is going to come to wealth is a slice of white pork for supper. That's what I should have said instead of just listening. How long does he think he can exist on dreams? Sees himself on a throne, crowned Emperor Magnus, pouring jewels through his fingers. He's blind. On the other hand maybe he's blinded himself deliberately. If that's true, he's more realistic than I am. Odd that he seems to be so much at peace, never angered. Who's blind? Yes, Summerfield, yes, there it is! Who was blind enough to lend McAuliffe money? Did Magnus? No. Earl Summerfield did. Now it's gotten so I'm even afraid to ask him for it because I know what he'd say. Oh man! Come on!—I haven't got it! Oh man!—don't bug me! So then I'd feel guilty for asking & probably would apologize, timidly touch his arm and smile. Don't want to offend anybody. I guess I'm more worried about offending somebody than about anything else. Fensdeicke comes around to "suggest" this or that—giving me an order is what it amounts to, and right away I start to explain and apologize. She never does that with McA—oh no, she Adores him, dirty cheap bastard—why doesn't she realize what he is. He treats HER like an inferior, she loves that. Maybe I ought to watch him, learn how he gets away with everything. I think it's just his manner, negligence, as if he didn't care whether or not he was fired. And I do care, that's what's wrong—trying to do a good job. Yes, there's my mistake.

I don't know. Maybe wrong. Feel confused and sick. My life's crumbling, flaking apart.

MARCH 26

Last Tuesday was B's birthday, just now thought of it. Of course she's been vicious—my fault. But why

74

couldn't she have reminded me? She'd rather nourish her hatred of me, only then is she satisfied. Thirty-four years old. She looks every year of it. She could be taken for forty, especially when she's irritated. Flesh like cheese. Also spiteful, vindictive. Doesn't trust me. "Earl, did you lock the door? Please go and look, somebody could walk right in." One of these days I'll strangle her. Why doesn't she Learn! The reason of course is that she's insensitive. Never notices how I respond. The other night turning the pages of the newspaper—making more & more noise. Did she pay any attention? Kept on talking, standing directly in front of me. Any normal person would take the hint. And the things she accuses me of. There's some truth in part of what she says. I'd be the last person to insist I was perfect. But when have I criticized her? Never. Not once. Oh—I've indicated how I felt, then what? She ignores me. I can't talk back to her in an argument, it's useless, not able to express myself as well as she does. Then if I don't say a word it seems to enrage her, more so than if I speak. Last month felt my throat contracting & was unable to answer when she asked a decent question, blood rushing through my head like a waterfall. Had the feeling I was about to do something but have no idea what, fortunately it subsided. May have been fortunate for us both. Right now I'd like to break something. Nervous & excited. Anything. How could I have forgotten? Maybe she didn't notice—hasn't said a thing about it. That's possible. What should I do? An apology could make the situation worse. I'd better keep quiet.

MARCH 27

Mexican girl kidnaped from playground near Mission Street, not seen since. McA claims there's a white slave trade flourishing in that district. My guess however is just that she was taken for private use, same as Lengfeldt. Seems as though it happens about once a month. Well, she's got a haughty face, most of them do. They look like they're ready to slap you or spit on you. Wherever she is she probably isn't feeling quite so proud. Nor is there a trace of sweet Loretta. Parents keep promising a reward for information, etc. It's all very familiar, familiar as an old play, only surprising thing is that the audience is always astonished.

Cloudy. Radio predicts rain tonight.

MARCH 28

Pfee-Pfaw. Life's tedious. I'm feeling fagged. What would it be like living in London? I might enjoy that, also might be more successful there. One thing I don't like about the United States is the suspicion. After work crossing 10th and stopped to chat with the policeman who's been there every day for years. Seemed natural, a friendly thing to do. I'm positive he knows my face but he just dropped his arms and stared at me, whistle gripped like a bone in his teeth. Occurred to me that I was interfering with traffic or some such and could be arrested if he wanted to, so scuttled off. I know he was busy, all right & I interrupted—it's just that—oh, I don't know what's wrong, nothing. Feeling sick and tired, that's all. Should try to make some friends. Get acquainted with more people. Too often alone. Might as well be wearing an iron mask.

MARCH 29

Followed some waitress in green uniform to 8th where she went into a building. Discovered her watching me as I hurried by the entrance. I kept going. How did she know I was following her? How do they always know?—I never got too close. She must have noticed my reflection in a store window. One glance was enough. Keep going Earl. On the other hand it's easy to misinterpret expressions. At the Bureau they assume I'm bored when in fact I'm deeply interested in something, therefore what I interpreted as a look of panic might actually have been an invitation. I ought to have stepped into that entrance and waited to see what she'd do. La-dee-da! It's too late now, but I'll look for her again, she must work somewhere in that neighborhood. One of those dirty little lunch counters. I'd like to make a chart of female habits.

Another week's ended & I feel encouraged. Not so despondent. I have reason to be hopeful.

MARCH 30

Bianca woke up early this morning, sat on the edge of her bed smoking. I pretended to be asleep. She belched and I had the impression she was a man. I must have been very nearly asleep. I thought that I was a woman. I thought that I was the wife & this was comforting. He'd be making the decisions, all the responsibility was his. Didn't want to open my eyes, didn't want to face the world once again, wanted only to have somebody care for me. Then I'd be privileged to wait for life instead of seeking it out.

B's more masculine than I am. She's always positive, decisive. I've never seen her hesitate. She never cries. I've watched her unfold the newspaper, fold it into the shape she wants. Seeing her do that makes me uncomfortable. She knows it—that's why she does it. Little pearls of contempt in her eyes. As if being born with testicles should make me what I'm not. All right, I'm not much of a man, who's to blame? She stares at me, shrugs, goes on smoking her cigarette and my backbone might as well be made out of spa-ghetti. Why did I get married? I must have known what she was. From the first instant I saw her I must have known. Yes, and she knew what I was.

I ought to quit the Bureau, that would be a way out. Get a different job. That would give me the confidence I lack. Yes, do that. And before long because somehow I know I don't have very much time.

MARCH 31

This Sunday afternoon to Lincoln Park. Asked if she'd like to go but she just shook her head, continued reading whatever it was—I think it was an article on stock-market profits. I have an idea she's planning to invest in some petroleum company, judging from those folders lying around. Well, it's her own money but I should think she'd discuss it with me, as a matter of courtesy if nothing else. A slight indication that she respects me, but I suppose that's expecting too much. I hope she loses every cent. Oh God if only I thought she had some use for me.

Now late at night, I look at my hands in the lamplight and am wondering at their emptiness. God has given us hands in order to grasp life, but what do I have? What sort of a beg-gar am I?

APRIL 1

On the roof for a while this evening to look at the moon and stars. Wish I had a telescope. Maybe I could buy one, small price to pay for feeling close to the immensity of space. To be able to watch the planets whirling around— guess you'd realize exactly how small people are, even the ones that have all the power. Bank presidents and so forth, don't amount to a thing. Dirty, greedy, selfish. Contrast compared to Infinity. What a contrast. All right, why not buy a telescope? Plenty in the pawn shops. 6th street and elsewhere. I could spare a few dollars. Would B object? She wouldn't see any sense in it but I don't need to tell her. Even if I decide not to buy one I could go in and look. Good, that's settled.

So here's another Monday finished. Only interesting news was about M. St. J. getting engaged. Should have kept the picture of her but just seeing her face began making me angry, crumpled it up and threw it down the chute. Planning to get married to Harold somebody.

Went down to the basement & got the paper. Harold Schenke. Graduate student at the university, studying business, also is Pacific Coast handball champion. Probably a musclebound fool with money going to inherit his father's business, belongs to the right clubs and all the rest of it. I

79

know the type. I've seen them often enough. Handsome snobs with everything on a silver platter, don't have to work for a living. I don't need to be told much about him to know what he's like. Remember walking around on Nob Hill a few weeks ago, seeing those High Society people come out of the Fairmont Hotel. Wanted to go up and shout my name in their faces, but of course they'd be right and Earl Summerfield would be wrong. Police wouldn't bother to ask questions. One look & they'd know. Sick of it. Sick of it. Sick of it!

APRIL 2

Rain. Laborers coming into the Bureau felt guilty about leaving tracks on the linoleum. How clumsy they are! Difficult for me to keep from smiling.

As for news, Chronicle full of the usual. A murder on Clement—husband came home from work and discovered his wife's corpse on the bathroom floor, clothing slashed to ribbons, house ransacked, etc. And up in Larkspur a bunch of thugs beat a schoolboy to death for no reason. Down in Argentina some political bigwig assassinated. Africa bristling with guns. Truth of the matter is that the world's too dangerous to think about. Only item that I liked had to do with charming Loretta Lengfeldt—another picture, description. Still missing. Appeal for information. Anybody seen this child? Well, I could offer a hint or two. Why do they pretend they don't know what's happened? They act as if she was still alive. I ought to call the Lengfeldts and tell them to wake up. Would they believe me? Probably not, go on believing what they want to believe until the evidence is uncovered. I ought to tell them anyway. However, they might have the call traced. Well, go to a booth several blocks from here. Could do that. I'm not a fool. Sometimes I just wonder why it is that everybody takes me for a fool or a Nobody. The kind that a big shot hands his hat to. Well, they're going to get a surprise one of these days.

APRIL 3

Very strange experience in the office this P.M. Had the feeling for a few seconds that somehow I'd been mysteriously transferred to a completely different part of the globe. Didn't alarm me—no, just felt dreamy & I guess bemused, content to watch. Sleep of the outer senses. A strange dreaminess came over me & I was indifferent. Overheard McAuliffe talking to Clegg about a pay raise for government employees and it occurred to me we weren't in San Francisco but in Leningrad. I don't know why Leningrad instead of Moscow for instance, but Leningrad it was. And all those laborers standing in line patiently watching us were Russian peasants. Signs on the wall were Russian and without actually thinking about it I knew I lived in an apartment building full of Russian workers, and had a bad-tempered redhaired Russian wife who taught school. Everything I looked at was Russian, also everything I owned and what I believed in. Remember that I thought about the United States as a strange deadly nation on the opposite side of the world. Was curious about it, as though I didn't know anything at all about it. Next remember lifting my head in order to look at the fluorescent light overhead because somebody was concealed above it, or some sort of device was up there making a record of my movements and my words. McA was talking just then but his voice had a foreign sound—I couldn't understand a word. He was talking but just uttering senseless noises. Also there were the numbers. Numbers and identification plates with names etched on them, papers rustling, etc. the same as always. Had an urge to turn around and glance at the clock because I wanted to know what time it was, but I wasn't bold enough. Mrs. Fensdeicke was there in back of me. If I turned around I'd meet her eyes and it might go on my report. Well, maybe the whole thing lasted half a second or maybe five or six seconds—I'll never know. Suddenly McAuliffe was speaking English again, then I heard my own voice explaining State regulations in regard to unemployment compensation to the peasant in front of me. I think he was a drill-press operator. No, that one came next. Remember now it was an unskilled laborer because his card had been filled out by somebody else. He couldn't write his name. Remember beckoning Clegg to come over and witness the X. In fact maybe that was what started my dream—knowing he was illiterate. I've never quite gotten used to the fact. California, United States of America, earning more money than I was but couldn't sign his own name. It makes me mad every time I think about it. How many times have I asked myself what's the point of working at the Bureau when I could earn a lot more as a hod carrier. Maybe decided that for once I wasn't going to let it bother me. I don't know, anyway there he stood and just holding the pen between his fingers was an effort. Clegg and I watched him finally draw his X, then sent him on his way. Yes, that was the cause, I'm sure of it. Thought to myself this can't be real. What I'm doing isn't real, this office isn't real, nothing is. I've got to be somewhere else.

APRIL 4

Still thinking about yesterday, at noon asked Magnus if he ever felt afraid to turn around & glance at the clock & he admitted he was. Said he had the idea of buying a little clock to put on the counter but was afraid to. Fensdeicke would know he was using it as a crutch to get through the day and would "suggest" he get rid of it. M's right, of course, that's what she would do. In fact she'd notice an extra pencil on the counter. Well, I'm positive she notices Clegg hauling that silver turnip out of his vest eighty times a day but she never says anything to him. I guess he's been there so many years nobody dares bother him. I don't intend to earn the same "privileges" but am getting anxious about my promotion. There should be word very soon. I don't want to think about what would happen if I don't get it. It's been so long already. I never expected to be living like this —this dusty creaky smelly old wooden apartment, everything falling to pieces, myself included. Rusty fire escape outside the window, car fumes from that parking lot across the street, pigeons waddling along the ledge of the building opposite, liquor store at the corner, laundry, cut-rate cleaners, second-hand clothing—what a neighborhood. Drugstore, Chinese grocery, gas station, barber shop, and those two vacant stores filled with used furniture—yes, and I could walk from here to Pacific Heights in twenty minutes. There's irony for you, Earl! Decent life waiting for me twenty minutes from here. It's that close! It's that close to me & I can't get to it. Sometimes have a feeling that people actually are trying to prevent me. Nobody—nobody in particular, but everything's arranged in layers so you can't get up. I deserve a lot more than this and I intend to get it, too. I'm not going to flake away like these people around me. I'll apply for membership in some expensive club. That's the first step up. Lead a more active life than I do. Try to make friends with important people in financial district. I could stop by some of those cocktail lounges after I get off work and have a drink with them. Yes, I'll do that. I've kept to myself too much. I've been keeping to myself body & soul. Might as well sit here holding my breath.

83

APRIL 5

Sinking into the muck at the bottom of a lake. Felt like this since I was born, but after all what does it matter? Does anybody care? Suppose I carved a hole in my forehead and staggered through the streets of San Francisco blinded by my own blood—who'd notice! Shit. What a life. Saving dimes and quarters.

APRIL 6

Tried to get into Bianca's bed last night but she lay still as a ghost. Why is it that all my attempts are ruined? Because I'm not worthy of love? Why doesn't she try to help me?

APRIL 7

Palm Sunday. I have trouble remembering what it's all about, can't say exactly why.

O Lord: who now in this way forms the offspring of our Death, being able with a gentle hand to blunt the thorns, which were excluded from Thy paradise? Thy omnipotency is not far above us, even when we have gone down much below.

APRIL 8

End of Mr. Lesso's 30-day reprieve. I suspect the Authorities were embarrassed about getting rid of him so close to Easter & were planning to give him another little reprieve until the holidays were over. At least that's what I read between the lines, but somehow there was one of those humorous mix-ups—telephone operator connected the governor with a lumberyard up in the redwoods and by the time they got it straightened out the pellets were in the pan. Execution itself must have been quite a spectacle. One of the reporters lost his lunch. Lost his breakfast, properly speaking. 10:03 A.M. Would like to witness an execution but am glad I missed that one. Description a bit grisly. Anyhow, he's gone for good. Probably deserved it, have forgotten what he did to get himself on Death Row, no concern of mine thank goodness. Frankly I don't care who's killed. For all I care they could substitute a reporter—now wouldn't THAT make a story. He'd probably deserve it too. Might as well do a thorough job while we're about it, line up the citizens like they did in Germany, get rid of about 30 million people in the United States and it would be a better place. I'd like to set fire to San Francisco and hope it swept across to the tip of Maine. Purify this stinking country.

APRIL 9

One day after Lesso's exit from the scene but I can't say his execution accomplished much if it was intended as a warning to the rest of the population because at 2 o'clock this A.M. somebody telephoned the Oakland precinct station and suggested a squad car go to a certain address. They found the front door open, went in and discovered 23-year-old secretary for an insurance company kneeling beside her own bed, hands & feet tied with nylon stockings, face smeared with blood. They cut the stockings, wrapped her in a blanket and drove to a hospital. She says a flashlight shining in her eyes woke her up and there was a man wearing white gloves and carrying a butcher knife who made her take off her nightgown and then tied her in that position. My guess is that he didn't take off his gloves during the operation because he didn't want to get his hands dirty by touching her. Didn't want to soil himself. Pursuit and annihilation of Evil. Antagonism of the Male by the female —the latter All Devouring.

APRIL 10

This noon in elevator very preoccupied—red silk dress, odor of lilac, thoughtful blue eyes. Elevator started up— Acted like it threw me off balance. Apologized. Felt the nubbin & metal circlet of a garter but she didn't say one word. I knew she wouldn't, thinking it might have been an accident. Is it, or not? She can't decide, by then it's too late. Well, so far I haven't been wrong about a single one, although I ought to be more cautious. This one today was scared. Puzzled, naturally, but also I could see the panic in her eye. The body told the truth, I was just saved by the argument of her mind. Caution.

APRIL 11

Why do I allow people to abuse me?—terrified by thought of asserting myself. I avoid arguments, turn aside, agree it's my fault, gaze at the floor, sick with disappointment, uncertainty. Why can't I be like the others? In fact, what AM I? McAuliffe borrows money promising to pay it back in a few days, but does he? Why don't I ask him for it? He'd look at me with contempt. He might not even bother to answer—just leave me standing there. He might signal the others and then dare me to ask for it again in front of everybody. In that case what would I do? How am I going to get my money back? He knows he can make a joke of me, knows I never DO anything. Of course the fact that he's never mentioned the debt could mean that he's simply forgotten all about it, so I shouldn't overlook that possibility. I ought to remind him. Mention it very casually as though I just happened to remember. If he'd just make some reference to it—then I could bring up the subject. As it is, every day my position grows weaker.

Certain times I'm sick to death of my own decency.

APRIL 12

Bureau closed on account of Good Friday.

APRIL 13

First time I've gone into a house. Nobody knew & what's the harm? I was restless, waves pounding against me. Am better now. Hadn't planned to do it, only meant to go for a walk. Walked & walked. I must have walked for at least two hours. Yes, at least that much. Walking along thinking about different things and stopping to look in windows. Every house I looked into there were people sitting in front of television & felt like I wanted to shoot them. I don't know why it—oh, well, what's the use going on like this! Learn to control my temper. Keep away from things that make me angry. Withdraw from wasted contact. Don't allow Self to become infected. There I was dancing around in somebody's back yard but no idea how I got there. Clothesline in my hand. Not sure what happened after that. Next remember climbing over a wooden fence and running as fast as the wind. I guess I could have scaled the side of any building in the world, my fingers felt like hooks. Running and running and never short of breath, agile as a mouse. I could hear myself breathing, breath rushing in and out of my lungs, but at the time it didn't matter. I was expecting dogs but met not a one. If so, I'd have looped a clothesline around his neck, the end of Mr. Dog. I suppose they were inside or asleep so didn't hear me. Don't know whose house that was, or how I knew the back door was unlocked, but I did know. I wasn't the least surprised when I turned the knob and it swung open. I walked right in, I just walked right in! Voices in the front room, I didn't stay long. Noticed a pair of pliers on the drainboard, so put them in my pocket and walked out. Seems to me I did something else in the kitchen but I can't remember what. Anyway, it's done, a matter for the past. Three hours ago, it might as well be three years.

APRIL 14

Easter. Today I imagined I had the Sign of the Cross tattooed on the soles of my feet. I was arrested and when they asked me what it meant I replied that in this way I mock Jesus Christ by trampling upon Him with every step.

APRIL 15

On the whole feeling cheerful this evening and have been thinking that I ought to take up a hobby—perhaps learn to play a musical instrument. If only I'd not been so stubborn as a child, can't recall how many times Aunt Ollie urged me to take the violin, but no, I was worried that somebody would laugh. I could be playing right now. My fingers are supple. I do have graceful hands, beautiful hands, wish more people noticed. I don't think many people notice hands but I always do. B's for instance—long and leathery. One could say that I possess the woman's touch, she has the man's. Odd. Also, how many times have I wished I could stay here and do nothing but cook, sew, etc. Envy them, resent their easy life, no need to make decisions. People say men have a better life but they don't know what they're talking about. I've always hated decisions, suppose that's why B and I came together, so impressed by her brisk personality. What was it about me that appealed to her? She says I'm helpless. I guess that's what she liked. Helpless! But of course she's right. I've never accomplished anything. Ran to her with news of expected promotion, hoping for approval! "That's fine, Earl, but don't bother me now. Can't you see I'm busy?" Yes, I see. All right, I know better than to sift those ashes.

APRIL 16

Last night she summoned me—our first affair in weeks. Not much doubt she despises me, despises herself for being forced to call me, however the body does insist. I did my best. Can't say it was much. And I'm rewarded with a brisk pat on the back. Then she ruffled my hair, what little's left. I'm going to be bald before the age of 30.

Sit here wondering how she'd act if we had children. No telling. She hasn't mentioned it for so long. Three years? I can't remember. It's as though there weren't any children in the world. Yet when we first got married I used to watch her face whenever there was a child nearby. Something would come over her. She seemed more at ease. I've noticed that with other women—even the old ones. I've tried to enter into it, but can't.

In any case the purse has been opened & found empty,

now she needs revenge. That night Spach came over for dinner, afterward she told me to move the lamp. It was all right where it was but she knew I'd be forced to get down on my knees. As though it's my fault we don't have children. "Earl, would you mind moving the lamp? I believe the light's bothering Mr. Spach." It wasn't & he said so. All three of us knew it wasn't bothering him, only Spach didn't know why she told me to move it. I should have had the courage to tell him, she'd have looked like a fool. Instead I glanced at the lamp as though to determine whether it was true. As soon as I did that I was lost, it meant I was going to agree. Both of them watching me kneel on the floor. Why did I do it? Why? My head under the table trying to find the socket. Well, there are ten thousand methods of revenge. I had mine. Stuck my blubbery arse in their direction. Spach may have thought I was just awkward, Bianca knew. I may be awkward but I know what I'm doing. She understood. Oh yes, no doubt of that. I could sense it. She got stiff as a honeycomb. Wasn't expecting me to behave insolently. She thinks she's sucked the spirit out of me. She assumes I'm dry as a beetle husk dangling in her web. Perhaps.

APRIL 17

Tonight at dinner she let me know that if anything else happens she's going to call the police—her pleasant Thank You for the other evening, at least that's my guess. Would like to open my sweet wife up with a flashlight & discover what's feeding inside. Maggots. Roaches. No other explanation for the way she treats me. Puts me in mind of those devices they used to have for women—braces, bridles and so forth. Halters to put around their neck. Remember reading what they did to that one who poisoned her husband—smeared her arms and legs with tar, made her stand on a barrel next to the stake—some kind of pulley arrangement, etc. and then at the signal somebody kicked over the barrel and somebody else lit the fire. She burned a long time—screaming and wriggling. Well, suppose dear Bianca gets rid of me what would happen to her? Not much. Maybe a few years in prison, maybe not even that because they'd accept every word she said. She's so Respectable. Who'd believe she'd kill anybody? But she is. Every morning it begins.

APRIL 18

Home early from work claiming a headache, which was the truth although not so bad I couldn't have put up with it until 5. Just that I had to get away from people. Out of sight. Away from so much noise. Also away from Fensdeicke criticizing me. I don't know what I did wrong but she was after me all day. Well, I've had enough criticism, just about all I can take! It's lucky I know how to control my temper. People take me for the mildest little fellow on earth. What would they say if I walked into that office tomorrow with a gun?

APRIL 19

Another Friday, another ugly moment with Bianca. If she'd been tactful and spoken reasonably I wouldn't have been forced to defend myself. Didn't intend to tell a lie, didn't want to, but as usual she left me no escape. Maybe the noise all day—horns outside the window for eight hours, gabbling voices, arguments, whistles, that crash of glass shattering this A.M. Then this noon hearing the newscast, Russia and America threatening each other with annihilation. Well, if I had some sort of animal between my knees I'd have slit its throat and thrown the blood at Heaven. Peace and silence, is that asking too much? Drums & horns inside my skull. My own wife shouting into my face that I'm filthy, upset me so much I probably danced a jig—can't remember. I don't want to remember. I don't want to think. Don't want anybody interfering with me. If they do, watch out! That's all I've got to say.

Noisy as late as it is! Truck grinding along the boulevard, brakes squealing. Would it do any good if I shouted?

Went into the kitchen, had a bite to eat and am somewhat calmed. I tend to excite myself unnecessarily, accomplishes nothing. Maybe the result of knowing I'll spend my entire life at the Bureau perched on a stool. One day I'll press both hands to my heart, look startled & that'll be the last of Earl Summerfield. By that time B will have worked into an important position, member of the Board of Education probably. Madame Superintendent we were terribly shocked to learn of the death of Mr. Summerfield. Ah—just what profession was he in? Then how will you explain me, Bianca? Are you going to let them know I spent my life asking the same questions again and again? Hardly dignified enough for the husband of the Superintendent of Education. However, you'll think of something. You always know what to say & how to say it. I know you Bianca—I know you better than you know me.

APRIL 20

Out most of this Saturday in order to avoid another situation over those two girls. Wasn't much doubt that if I stayed home there'd be trouble. Just the same I let them know I was here. Caught them getting into the elevator. Bumped against the tall one & then asked how the lessons were coming along. She didn't say anything, just looked at her friend. Both of them wearing mascara, the young bitches, can't wait. And their hair piled up—both of them ought to be fucked & whipped. I'd beat them within an inch of their lives, teach them not to run around the streets looking like ten-cent whores. They make me sick, both of them.

Well, then what? Think, Earl, think. After the elevator, what? Outside, hands shaking so I couldn't light a cigarette. Got on the first bus, rode along with eyes shut. That must have been 2 o'clock. Tried to quiet down by reading a movie magazine somebody left on the seat and then—hmm, remember being in the Mission district and stopping at a drugstore for a dish of ice cream. Was feeling better by that time although still trembled. I probably wandered up Mission or maybe across—oh yes, saw the sign at Army so I was there. Not much else comes to mind until late afternoon —in the aisle of some church talking to the minister. His face was as blank as a paper mask. I'm not sure what we talked about, can't recall a single word he said. The world's in a bad way if people like that are supposed to give us spiritual instruction.

APRIL 21

Sunday. Thinking about my vacation. And of course about the promotion. Should be hearing very soon. All in all, a nice day today.

APRIL 22

McAuliffe's been accused of theft! Not quite true because am exaggerating, one of my bad habits. However I'm pretty sure that's what it was all about, couldn't be any other explanation. Fensdeicke went into Mr. Foxx's office as soon as those checks were reported missing, then the only person sent for out of our department was McAuliffe, which means he's under suspicion at the very least, even though I don't know how he could have managed to steal them since he doesn't have anything to do with disbursement. But he did it. I'm sure. He's guilty. He's just the type. Stories about him stealing tips off of cafeteria tables. Probably true. Doesn't care about anybody except self. Take anything from anybody whether he had any use for it or not. He's rotten inside, smells like a barrel of garbage. Eyes watery from liquor. Oh, yes, he's a pretty sight! I'd bet my soul he's guilty.

Also, I've got something else to consider. He still hasn't paid me my $20. Suppose he really IS guilty, then if they convict him of stealing those checks he'll be jailed & I won't have any chance of getting what he owes me. All right, I'll give him a while to recover from what happened in Foxx's office this morning, then approach him about the debt. No sense letting it continue.

APRIL 23

Approached him this P.M. about it with no result but right now that doesn't matter!—he told me it's true we're going to have a new super beginning the first of next month and I am the one! Said he heard Foxx say so yesterday to Fensdeicke. Apparently that conference wasn't about him stealing checks after all. I was unfair. I'm too quick to suspect the worst of people. McA is very decent. Not that I intend to let him get away indefinitely without paying me back what he owes me, but there could be plenty of reasons he hasn't been able to so far. Debts. I don't know much about him. Every day practically side by side but can't say I know really who he is. If he wants to squander his money

94

drinking that's his business. He's always been nice to me, has always said hello in the morning. In fact he's the only one who seems glad to see me. Also, little favors he's done that I take for granted. This promotion for instance—he didn't need to tell me, but he did. Told me it's settled. First of May there'll be a second supervisor in the office—Earl Summerfield! Have to pinch myself. Pinch again! Earl Summerfield! My God my God—and even Bianca was pleased. Didn't that come as a surprise to her! Stared at me as though I'd gone out of my mind, but once she realized I wasn't joking it was pretty clear she was impressed. Didn't anticipate promotion for her husband. Refused to believe me when I said I was expecting it. Well, she does now!

Oh Christ how I needed this! Nobody knew. I didn't know myself how much I've needed this. I was almost out of my head with rage and disappointment. Everything I've put up with. Kicked back & forth. Insulted. Cheated. My work ignored or just "accepted." Nobody ever complimented me. Nobody ever told me they thought I was a pretty nice person or that I was worthwhile. No. Just complete silence. Living in a closet. Had begun to decide Magnus was right—put your trust in hidden bags of gold, Ouija boards, etc. Had begun to think that my virtues such as patience and not complaining about being overlooked didn't mean much any more. But they do! Finally. Finally. Finally.

Well, things are adding up, no doubt about it. Fensdeicke glancing at me this afternoon, smiling. Hadn't paid much attention but now I see why. She's recognized me as an equal. I wonder when I first was noticed by Mr. Foxx. Might be when I had that dizzy spell—and there's Fate for you! If I hadn't got sick that day, who knows? In any case I've always liked & respected Foxx, and do not believe McA's dirty stories about him. I think he's a very distinguished · man. He's probably of West Indian descent or something like that. Would guess he had a British ancestor, because he

doesn't seem at all like those uneducated black laborers I have to put up with half the day. Now only one more week of it—a week from tomorrow I report for work as a Supervisor. I just can't quite believe it! No more sitting like a duck on a stool. I'd better train myself to begin thinking of Mrs. Fensdeicke in first-name terms. It'll soon be "Good morning, Earl!" Then I believe I'll look a little bit amused and surprised and I'll say to her, "Oh!—good morning, Sara."
A wonderful day.

APRIL 24

Had a dream this morning & woke up an instant before it ended. Thought somebody was standing at the foot of the bed gazing down at me. I was sure I heard somebody ask my name, just then opened my eyes and noticed a figure hurrying into the closet. Not sure if I was awake or asleep—it's hard now to remember. Have a feeling I ran across the room and jerked open the closet door. Of course nobody was inside, nothing except the usual things. There I stood in my pajamas looking at that old suit I wear to the office. I guess living the way I've lived has affected me. I don't dare count how many nights I've sat here at the desk and done nothing but stare up the hillside through the telephone wires to those big apartments on top of Pacific Heights. I've been afraid to go for a walk up there—afraid I'd be arrested. That's how afraid I've been. But it's all over now. Mysterious currents draw a man up or down.

APRIL 25

Here it is already Thursday. Should be hearing the news officially by tomorrow, Monday at the latest.

Strange that McA himself doesn't seem the least bit interested in getting a promotion. I suppose he realizes he couldn't, not with his attitude and poor record. Sat down on the grass to eat his lunch that time we went outside last week. Everybody else obeyed the sign but he stepped over the chain, sat down, took off his shirt to enjoy the sunshine as if he was in his own back yard. People staring but he didn't pay any attention, went right on eating his lunch, drinking coffee, belching, scratching his stomach. He's never had any respect for regulations, but he will after I'm a super. He won't get away with things like that. I intend to make several changes in the department, reorganize procedures, work toward better efficiency, eliminate a few unnecessary expenses. Quite a bit of time wasted around the office in various ways, odd Mrs. Fensdeicke doesn't notice it. Among the first things I'll do is point that out to her & make my recommendations, invite her to discuss them with Mr. Foxx and me.

APRIL 26

Another week of work finished. Not a word from Foxx. He must be planning to surprise me. My guess is that everybody else in the office has been told about it but was asked to keep quiet. Possibly they're planning a party for me. After work next Tuesday—the end of the month. If they're going to have a party that would be the time. Don't know. Maybe I'm expecting too much. I won't count on it.

APRIL 27

Saturday hanging around the wharf. Summer's approaching. Tourists with cameras, etc. Lobster boiling in the pots, picture postcards in racks outside the restaurants, sidewalk artists, also there's a new wax museum—guess I haven't been to the wharf in quite a while because somebody said the museum's been there almost six months. Occurs to me I haven't been enjoying the city very much. Too much time inside this one room. I'll get out more often. Haven't visited the zoo since when? Don't have any friends except at the Bureau. Never go to night clubs, not even ball games. However I'll start Living pretty soon. For instance, band concert tomorrow & could go to that. Or visit art galleries. In fact I could buy some paints myself—that's become very popular the last few years. I know I could paint some beautiful pictures. I could paint the cable cars and the bridges, put them up on the fence there at the wharf and might sell a few. I know I could paint as well as some of those I saw this afternoon. Most of them looked like a child did them. Any number of ideas popping into my head!

Well, that's that for today. I'm looking forward to next week.

APRIL 28

Sunday. Slept late. Bianca was out somewhere when I woke up. I was going to ask if she felt like us doing something together, but she didn't leave me a note so I went out at 4 P.M. Managed to waste the day, as usual. I seem to do it in spite of myself. Ordinarily I'd be exasperated about wasting another Sunday but ever since McA let me in on the news I can't get really angry with myself. This is a milestone of my life. Could say I've been wandering around in a swamp, or quicksand—that's how I feel, but finally am steady on my feet. Yes, much to look forward to.

APRIL 29

At the Bureau they acted as though I didn't exist.

APRIL 30

The new supervisor will be somebody from another office—another woman. Her name's Anurein or Annerin. She starts work tomorrow. It was just one of McAuliffe's jokes. How much longer am I going to deceive myself? I know people are dirty, so why do I go on believing them?

Take a good look at yourself, Summerfield. If you thought you were unimportant before please look at yourself now. How do you like it?

Try once more to sleep.

MAY 1

Just a few days ago everything made sense, now I can't even remember why I expected a promotion. They must be laughing at me behind my back. I could sit on that stool fifty years without being noticed. What's happened to Clegg will happen to me. Occasionally I'll get a pat on the head, enough to keep me enthused until it no longer matters —until I don't dare quit. So this is how it is—and I prided myself on doing neat work, never being late! I thought Mr. Foxx recognized me. Today I passed him in the corridor & spoke, he doesn't remember my name. He's seen my face before, that's all he knows about me. Well, God damn his soul! I pray that he goes blind, that his heart fails. I hope his tongue swells in his black throat so that he can never speak again. I've been told lies enough. Shit. I pray that the blood of his buggery black body runs out through every hole.

MAY 2

Took this afternoon off, told Fensdeicke I felt nauseated. I've never done such a thing before—have never lied to her. Went to a movie because I needed some darkness. Everybody stares at me as if I was made of glass.

Times I do feel transparent. Cannot endure it—if everybody keeps staring at me—what? I don't know. I get so discouraged. Comes from being cheated, I think. Knowing I don't really amount to much. I guess it's time I accepted the fact. Everybody uses me for his own selfish purpose, also a fact. Don't deny it.

Horns day & night! Doesn't do much good to cover my ears. Next the silence. Clock ticking across the room. Turn on the radio, learn what's happening outside.

News reports Alcatraz prison is Leaking. Leaking! Two convicts tunneled halfway through one of the walls with a spoon—a spoon! The place is collapsing, won't stand up much longer. Evil digs its way toward us. How soon is it going to reach us? Or is it already here but we haven't recognized it? I don't know. The world's gotten too big, complicated & dangerous. Voice of the Antichrist. Sand drifting over the walls of the city. Newscaster says America has developed some kind of new weapon powerful enough to destroy every form of life and authorities believe if it was used nothing could grow on the earth for at least a century. Strange that doesn't alarm me. My feeling is that if the end of the world's in sight, I don't care. I've had no part of it.

MAY 3

Past few nights wandering through the neighborhood hopping fences like a leopard. A nap after work & no need to sleep. Maybe I was born at night.

MAY 4

Saturday on the beach concealed in the sand. Scooped myself a nest, observed the gulls. How serene they

101

are, take up stations on the wind. Continents. Oceans. Space flies beneath them. Then come back to the apartment to Bianca's shrieks— "Where have you been! Oh you bastard!" All because I didn't stop by the cleaners to pick up her suit. Going to some political assembly in Millbrae tomorrow, now she can't wear that suit. Why does it matter? Why is it important? That's what I should have asked. However, didn't feel like arguing. Besides, admit she told me about it & told me not to forget. Apologized. Once again I've been wrong. Apologizing as I have a thousand times. Did she ever tell me she was sorry about anything? Oh no. Never. Not once in all these years. She makes me feel like her personal butler. Have had about all the insults I intend to take. Might mail her a little gift she doesn't expect—a strangled bird packed in cotton.

MAY 5

M. St. J. in the paper again. Picture of her at a fancy cocktail party on Presidio Terrace talking to some baldheaded old fart in a tuxedo, probably got twenty million dollars, but here I am—Earl Summerfield worth at least $600, counting everything in the closet. There's equality for you. Those dirty snobs.

Enjoy the day as best you can, Earl, because tomorrow you'll be back at work. Another week. January. February. March. April. Very different from the sort of life you'd lead if you were born in the right part of the city.

MAY 6

The new supervisor smiles too much. She's attempting to be friendly because she knows that job is rightfully mine. I understand that she didn't steal it from me, in fact I doubt if she had even heard about me until she was transferred to our department, but the fact remains that I ought to be in her position. We're both perfectly aware of this, even though neither of us has mentioned it. She's playing up to me. She's ashamed. "Earl, please call me Betty." Then she goes on about "unpleasant duties," etc. I don't know what she was leading up to, she concealed the meaning of her remarks as women often do. They can't be honest. Being what they are they can't help but attempt to degrade and humiliate and confuse other people. Well, I'm not easy to deceive. The next time she speaks to me I'll let her know I'd prefer to be addressed as Mr. Summerfield. There's no reason for us to be familiar. I shouldn't have been so obliging, now it'll be difficult to alter the situation. She caught me by surprise. The first thing that came into my head was that I ought to be pleasant to her, otherwise she could write up a nasty little report. So there was a smile on my face before I could catch it & I watched myself do everything but get down on the floor to lick her shoes.

Seems as though I've always always always been supervised by women. There's been some woman watching me since the day I was born. I don't think I'll ever get their talcum powders out of my nose, at times it feels like the inside of my skull is white or pink with talcum. How did they get so much authority? I don't mind if a man tells me what to do, I accept the fact that he's possibly a more valuable person than I am. I know my limitations. I'm not one of the smartest men on earth & don't pretend to be. Even here at the Bureau there's Mr. Foxx—no question about it, he's a very smart man, otherwise he wouldn't be in that position. Now if he'd give me an order I wouldn't hesitate a moment. I'd like to be his assistant. There's an idea. I wonder if anybody's thought of that. I might talk to him. I'm sure he could get permission from Sacramento to have somebody sharing his office as a kind of deputy. Plenty of special cases arise, problems of a particular nature that I'd be suited to handle. Even if a promotion didn't accompany it there wouldn't be any doubt of the status. That would put me at least on the level with Fensdeicke and Aneurine, slightly above them perhaps. They'd have to go through me in order to talk to Mr. Foxx. I could approve or disapprove of their requests. Yes, talk to Foxx about it toward the end of the week when we're not so busy—that's what I'll do. He'd welcome somebody to handle part of the work. I'm surprised he's never thought of it. Well, that'll be MY reward for thinking up the idea. As far as Aneurine is concerned, starting tomorrow I'll treat her formally & refrain from smiling. Simply say good morning Miss Aneurine, then hang up my coat, walk straight to my stool. I wonder what she'll make of that! It'll puzzle her, if nothing else. She'll realize something's going on. She'll take notice of me. I'll immediately stand out from the others. That'll be a good beginning. Yes, and later I'll stop to outline my proposal for Mr. Foxx. It should work out very well. Strange I didn't think of this before.

MAY 7

Vladimir quit work 3 minutes early this afternoon. Had nothing to do, no more applicants, so he simply walked to the cloakroom for his hat, stopped at the cooler for a sip of water, then out the door. Everybody watched him leave, not a word spoken. Nobody's done that before. If the lobby's empty we're supposed to pretend—examine cards, rearrange papers, something, anything, some sort of little movement. The Bureau doesn't want us to be idle. I don't know why it is, I'd never thought about it, but almost every evening I've filled up the last few minutes by pretending that I had something to do. Ever since I started to work

104

at the Bureau—yes, Magnus, McA, all of us, even old Clegg. Keep busy. No loitering. V is the first to be honest & admit the Bureau degrades us. I wonder if he'll get in trouble over it. When I realized that he was actually leaving I glanced at the clock, then at Fensdeicke. Her face was frozen. She knew everybody in the office was watching to see what she'd do. She didn't move a finger, not an eyelash. I think she was frightened. Nobody had ever done what V did, consequently she was paralyzed. 4:45 is when we get off our stools. I'm sure she was frightened. She didn't know what he was going to do if she tried to stop him. That must be the key to everything—if you break the law you've announced that you think the law is stupid. You've let people know that Authority can be stupid, it's why they're shocked and alarmed, it means that whoever's been obeying the law is equally stupid. Yes, no wonder Mrs. Fensdeicke behaved like that—quiet as a rabbit. I could almost see her thumping heart. Also, I think Vladimir perfectly estimated the time. Two minutes later and nobody would pay much attention, but two minutes earlier and I believe F would have questioned him, asked if he didn't have something to do. He chose the one moment to be effective. That means he doesn't want to lose his job. It means he wanted to show exactly what he thought but at the same time oh ho ho!—he didn't want to lose his job. I know how he feels.

MAY 8

People hate their superiors & plot against them. This is the reason Fensdeicke and Miss Aneurine talk about me. They both understand that I ought to be in a supervisory position. Both of them feel guilty about the fact that I'm officially subordinate to them. They know it should be the other way around. I mustn't blame them, they aren't responsible, although of course it's possible they've arranged to keep my record secret. I don't know who comes down from Sacramento to look over the personnel so it's difficult to say exactly what's going on, however the fact remains that our relationship is incongruous. Both of them should be my subordinates. They probably know how efficiently I'd run the office. I'd whip everybody, including themselves, into proper shape. I'd have a little cane, a flexible cane & give it to them right and left! Aneurine! Fensdeicke! Step up here, please. Very good. Now on your toes, if you please. Bend over. One-two & one-two! I'd give it to them until blood ran down their stockings. Then they'd be forced to admit who was master—there wouldn't be any doubt, not a bit! That's how to gain confidence. The world is pretty much a matter of Will. Strength overwhelms Weakness.

Yes, I'm feeling more confident. The only trouble is that I look like practically everybody else and I act the same. Nobody notices me. I'm indistinguishable. Could walk into Buckingham Palace if I had on the proper costume, or into Greenwich Village. How long has it been since anybody's seen me? Years, I guess.

I complain too much. The fact is, I'm extremely fortunate. Nothing's so valuable as good health. I don't get sick. My job's secure. I ought to give thanks. Perhaps all that troubles me is the monotony of life. That should be easily cured. I'll take a trip. Two weeks' vacation coming up. Let's see. Paper says the Kileau sails from San Francisco to Hawaii, Fiji, New Zealand, Australia, Philippines, Hong Kong, Japan, etc. Wouldn't THAT be something! The people at the Bureau would never get over it if Earl spent his vacation in—it would take too long, I don't have that much time. Maybe I could get to Hawaii. Of course there's flying. Time & expense. The thing to do is lay some plans. Next week I'll make a few telephone calls, inquire about reservations, tickets, etc., etc. I mustn't let Life get out of hand.

106

MAY 9

Moment of dizziness this noon & afraid I was about to fall. However, it passed. I don't believe there's anything wrong with me, except that I'm flabby. Have never felt Vigorous. The bathroom light makes me look fleshy & somewhat softer than I am. Lipstick and eyeshadow and a wig and I'd be complete. I'm eternally studying myself like a woman, wondering how to present myself to the best advantage. Generally, I think I approach life very much as they do, therefore shouldn't blame myself for small failures. Being a captive isn't unpleasant. Weakness can be gratifying, a sort of self-indulgence. I simply need more leisure in which to perfect my thoughts. There's so much to clarify. Days grow longer without the slightest benefit to me.

Almost 4 A.M. Attempted to sleep but was angered by Bianca's breathing. Also, cars & trucks going by, dog barking. Sat up awhile to observe street light shining on her face —the face of my lioness. Turned on her side & one soggy breast came pouring out of the gown, yellow, wrinkled, reminding me of an egg or a waffle. Fortunate she didn't wake, I wouldn't have been so docile. No arguments for me in the dead of night. Dressed, jacket & tennis shoes, climbed the back fence, tried a few doors. My head feels sensitive, as though I bumped into something, but I don't think so. Have no recollection of that. Will try again to sleep.

MAY 10

Groggy all day. I'm staying up too late. Last night dreamed of the bloody egg, a dream I've had before. Now it's just eleven, an hour I've never liked—I'm restless and unhappy, terribly alone, and last night's dream is oppressive. I'll stand in the closet for a little while to calm myself, then have a bowl of soup and go to bed.

MAY 11

Saturday & news I've been anticipating: Lori Lengfeldt's body in the traditional shallow grave. Head twisted & flung back—mouth yawning the final shriek, stuffed with dirt. On a gentle hillside near the beach. Preliminary evidence indicates she was assaulted, that's how they put the matter. I don't know what they've learned but a few details would be interesting. The pattern's extremely typical of America. One day the Innocent is missing, then the public starts to howl like monkeys in a burning forest. Always the same, every single time it happens! Well, I suppose they're taken in by their own lies. Now one's turned around to bite them, naturally they're bleeding, howling with anguish, prancing about eager to catch somebody and destroy him— as if that's going to stop it from happening tomorrow. Well, bugger the people and screw everything they believe. Mills of the gods grind slowly, but they never stop.

MAY 12

America the beautiful! Of course. Songwriter Jeremy Katz's fair lady divorced him yesterday in Beverly Hills. Tells reporters "We're still the best of friends!" as she goes home with a million-dollar settlement. She complained he stayed out late at night. Oh yes, from a distance nothing's wrong. Such purity, generosity, nobility of purpose. Then take a few steps closer, make sure you've got a clothespin on your nose. See America white with maggots, red with blood, blue with hypocrisy. Greed, suspicion, hate, scum, treachery. Police at every corner wearing a holster with a big pistol in it—proof enough! The Savior hasn't quite gotten around to us yet. Liberty? Abracadabra! Justice? When have you met it? Give me a description of its face. Decency? Everywhere you look. Reverend Alford Lusk, pastor of First Church of the Redwoods, got caught kneeling beside some woman's bedroom window but insisted he lost the keys to his car and was trying to find them. Everybody laughs, that's the sort of nation this is. I wonder just how funny He thinks it is! And the person actually responsible—she's pretending to be shocked, but the fact is she didn't pull the curtains quite together. She's the one that ought to be in jail. They ought to shave her body from top to bottom & drive her through the street!

Yes, the longer I think about things the clearer it all becomes. They're the cause. Great men of the past have been correct teaching contempt for them. They hand over their bodies to lechery & their brains to thoughts of petty revenge. Poisonous flowerbeds attracting us subtly to the grave. According to Leviticus they're beasts of burden. Vladimir once told me the Koran treats them with absolute scorn, and the commandments of Solon allowed them no rights whatsoever. Religion of Manu decided they were incurably vile and ought to be kept in slavery, etc. Whatever happens to them they bring on themselves. If they deserved trust and love of Man it's what they'd receive. Instead you have only to look at them and consider what they do! Watch their movements, every gesture's a lascivious invitation. I'm sick to death of being near them. See them climbing steps ahead of me & all I can do to keep from jamming something in to the hilt. Walking the streets—walking and mincing as they go. Enter thee into the rock and hide thee in the dust for fear of the Lord and for the glory of His majesty. The daughters of Man are haughty. Because they are haughty they walk with stretched necks and wanton eyes, walking and mincing as they go. But the Lord will smite the crown of the head and He will find their secret parts. Nobility of Man devoured by omnivorous flesh. Exposure, suggestion. Defiling whatever they touch.

MAY 13

Why doesn't Aneurine leave me alone! Just before noon today limping along the aisle and stopped to discuss my interviews. Heavy praise. Showed me the figures on her memo pad. "Earl, all of us are delighted with your work. You're doing so well." Thank you, Miss Aneurine, thank you. But what did she actually want to talk about? What is it she wants? Why does she interrupt me so often? Doesn't make sense. Middle-aged, forty at least. Then there's that leg. Accident or disease? Chafed & seems to be slightly reddened, skin thickened. Maybe she's lonely. Probably that's the reason. I'm sorry about it but there's nothing I can do, not a thing. Her voice bothers me, feeling she might collapse into tears at any moment. It's like music quivering out of an old Victrola trumpet. What does she want?

Might as well admit it. Don't even want to consider it, but I know what she wants. Wants me to come visit her some evening. If I did, what would she do for me in return?

MAY 14

Took a careful look at Aneurine. That's what she wants all right but have decided I couldn't do it. Not with her. It's not possible. I'd be soft as a lily, trying to hide my disgust. So would anybody. She ought to realize nobody

110

could care about her. She ought to give up the idea of love —it isn't necessary.

That's about all for this Tuesday. Notice that Bianca bought a couple of goldfish and a little aquarium. All right, they belong to her, I'm not going to take the responsibility of feeding them. If they die she won't be able to blame me. I won't even mention them.

MAY 15

Four minutes after 10 A.M. at work instead of in the apartment. Drinking tea instead of usual coffee. Seated at far end of the metal table in basement of the Bureau. One of the fluorescent lights overhead is flickering & buzzing. Just glanced at sign stenciled on the door saying this place for use of employees only. I know I belong here & yet everything's remote. There's a smell of electricity. Feels as though I'm in the execution chamber. 6 after 10. Other end of the table Fensdeicke & old Clegg talking. Upstairs the cattle stand patiently in double rows, stepping across the white line one after the other the instant McAuliffe or Vladimir beckons. Magnus is at home sick. Fensdeicke just noticed me writing—nodded, smiled, asked if I was writing an expose of the Bureau. I said of course & she laughed. I'm not usually witty, it's satisfying to cause people to laugh. Paying no more attention to me, still talking to Clegg. Now twelve after—I've got only 3 more. F knows to the instant when I'm due upstairs. She won't speak a word, but I predict that approximately 2 minutes from right now she'll glance at the clock. Not at me, but she'll turn her head deliberately so that I'll be forced to notice that she's looking at the time. Subtle way of telling me. Yes. That'll be the first hint, then I'll have a few seconds of grace. Before a full minute passes she'll look again, after which if I'm still here she'll smile once more, ask what time my break is over. I don't dare wait that long. Theoretically I could spend my entire fifteen minutes here, and in fact I actually could do it—perhaps once, maybe even twice—and be several seconds late returning to my stool. Yes!—there she glanced at the clock. We understand each other. 40 seconds. McA will be just about to close his window, feeling in his pocket for a cigarette—Aneurine watching him and V while F's watching Clegg and me. I'll meet McA on the steps 20 seconds from right now. Clegg on his feet. F restless, knows I'm cutting it thin. Time's up!

MAY 16

Worst night of my entire life, at least almost. Maybe it was, I'm still ready to puke. Felt like vomiting in her face. Why is it that if a woman hates a man she wants to get as close to him as possible? More she hates him the closer she gets—I think because she wants to be sure he's going to pay for it. Doesn't want him to escape. All I wanted was to get out of this place—as far away from her as I could. Didn't think she was ever going to stop, but I've heard it all before. Nothing she says can hurt me any longer. Besides, she's nothing but a bad-tempered bitch trying to humiliate me. Hasn't got anything except a hole below her belt, that's why & both of us know it!

Pfaw! Pfaw! Fiddle-de-dee. I'm all fagged out. Tongue feels thick as a tennis ball.

MAY 17

Got my hair cut after work. Reading a detective magazine in the barber shop. It said there were 7,000 murders in the U.S. last year, however only 65 murderers were executed. Thinking about it, must be easier to satisfy your need for revenge than most people believe. 65 out of 7,000. Also, that's considered the most serious crime. Ho ho! There's that much chance I'll fall and crack my skull in the tub. In fact, with those odds why not get rid of Bianca? Toss a noose over her head when she's filing her nails, count the pulse beats while she squirms around. Probably die the same as a bird, arms flopping and flailing like wings.

Quite cold tonight. Sunny and pleasant all day but while I was at the barber shop the fog rolled in, since then very cold, foghorns, ships moving cautiously. Seeing them float toward the Golden Gate makes me sad, reminds me of how I need to get away. Would love to go far away before it's too late. Too late? Why think that?

MAY 18

Saturday. Studying Dogs because it occurred to me they're more typical of us than we are of ourselves. Suspect it's possible to learn a great deal about people by observing dogs. Fensdeicke with her dugs hanging down to her waist. That bitch Aneurine with her scaley look, nosing around for scraps of food in a garbage can. Mr. Foxx trotting by looking at everybody with a buttery expression and his sideways glance—large old brown dog with swinging dick. McA, too, watched him messing up the sidewalk in front of our place, grunting, squeezing his hindquarters.

Yelped when I booted him, dirty mongrel. Oh every sort of person's represented and in one afternoon I saw practically everybody I know. Not many of them were beautiful.

That was about all I did today. Picked up tomorrow's Examiner for a change and first thing I saw when I unfolded it was a parade of women in bathing suits. What's become of female pride and decency?—that's what I'd like to know. Right at this moment in this apartment house and in the next one and the next and every building or house in the city you could find them hunching and contracting like eels. Dirtying the earth. Grease & rubber. Eggs, blood.

MAY 19

Salesman caught in the ladies' lounge at the airport. Insists he's innocent, went in wrong door by mistake. Hippity-hop! Wrong door, he says. Wrong door! Police think he might be the one who sliced up that nurse a few months ago in Mill Valley but I doubt it—doubt it very much, requires a different sort. Police probably know better, probably investigating him just to prove to the public that they're still after that dreadful Criminal. Oh yes. Always get their man if it takes a hundred years. Pfut! Little salesman, all he wanted was to look. My guess is he collects detective magazines and glossy pictures—girls in leather boots whipping each other, wrestling, tied to the bed, etc. He just likes to look, very simple. Should never have gotten outside his private world, ought to stay inside examining his collection, then he wouldn't get hurt. Now they'll ruin him. Stupid little man who thought real women would be more exciting than the pictures. Well, of course he isn't "stupid," must have a good imagination, otherwise he'd know pictures were only pictures. Anyway he bores me, he's just a ghost.

MAY

Ho hum! Everything rhythmic today but don't know why. Times when I almost swayed as I walked.

MAY 20

Monday. At lunch McAuliffe said Foxx has intercourse with one of the stenos—says it happens in Foxx's office. Certain types, says McA, get excited by thought of being discovered. Went on & on. Told him I didn't believe it. McA is trying to slander Mr. Foxx, that's my opinion. Unimportant people always attack their superiors, as I ought to know! Happened to me often enough. Looked around during the afternoon when that little Mexican tramp went into his office but could see only blurred figures behind the glass. True she did stay in there a long while, walked out with absolutely no expression & straight back to her typewriter. I don't know. I don't know. Rather not believe it. However I did get a feeling she stopped to fix her clothes before opening the door. Hmm. Yes. Believe I've changed my mind. In fact, am positive. Attempts at concealment always futile because we understand each other even when the brain doesn't want to admit it. Having admitted it, now I see! So it's actually been going on in Foxx's office! Pfft. Guess I should have realized. McA's right. I always give people credit for being better than they are.

Very enlightening thought. The good tree does not bring forth evil fruit, neither does the corrupt tree bring forth good fruit.

MAY 21

This afternoon walking toward McA's wicket with some reports when Aneurine stopped me, said I ought to walk more briskly. Was too amazed to reply, too amazed to think. First thing that occurred to me was to apologize, then explained I was going to give the reports to McAuliffe, etc. All over before could gather my wits. Aneurine with her milky smile, murmuring she was sure it wasn't going to happen again. "Mr. Foxx is interested in achieving peak efficiency." Then she turned around, walked away, left me standing there nodding, trying to explain even while she was walking away. Happened so fast, that's the reason. It startled me. And then of course to make matters worse I practically ran the rest of the way to McAuliffe. He snickered. He'd seen. So did everybody else in the office. Summerfield reprimanded publicly. And tonight just as if she'd found out about it Bianca asks how things are going at the Bureau. Probably somebody telephoned her because there isn't any other reason she suddenly took an interest in what I was doing. Standing there with her arms folded. "Earl, is something the matter with you?" What I should have answered was "Bianca, is something the matter with You?" However maybe it was best not to answer, it shows greater sophistication to remain silent after you've been insulted. On the other hand maybe I should have slapped her. Yes, I think that's what I should have done but it's too late now. Well, in a day or so I might bring up the subject and let her know exactly what sort of a day this was. Or I might not. It depends.

MAY 22

Vacation starts Monday after next but I still haven't made up my mind where to go. One thing's certain, I intend to get out of San Francisco for two weeks. Last year we went to Los Angeles for a few days but the place stinks of car fumes. I don't guess it's improved, probably worse. B hasn't said a word about us going anywhere together, just as well because she'd decide on some place I don't want to go. That's always how it's been. Not one year we went where I suggested. She decides. It's gotten so I have trouble deciding anything for myself. I don't know how I got into this situation. Well, yes, I think I do. All my life I had to be polite if it was a woman, give up my seat on the bus, etc. etc. What thanks did I get?

Yes, I think that's how it began & now there's no question. Do whatever I'm told. Ask what she wants me to get at the dime store or the drugstore, then wait until she decides. Ask if she feels like going to a movie. Or suppose I ask, "Bianca, how about going up to the redwoods for a while? We could rent a cabin. How about it?" Then I wait, wondering if she's going to say something to make me sound like a fool. No way out. Seems like there was a time but it's gone. I've been walking down the steps too long, impossible to turn around & start back up.

MAY 23

On the roof this evening noticed a couple of dresses, stockings, underwear pinned up to dry. Before I knew what was happening I had a little black piece of something stuffed in my pocket. Think it belongs to that one with the long hair who lives on the 6th floor beside the elevator. Anyway, put it in paper bag & locked it in my cabinet. Dread the thought of what a scene there'd be if Bianca discovered it. Pleasure from a rag—no sense denying it, am just trying to be honest with myself. Promise of a dream. Reality itself not half so real. Everything we see or smell or touch—last week seeing that peach sliced open in the kitchen and immediately thought about their Parts. How unexpected. Suppose only God knows what boils up from hidden depths. Same as it was tonight. Went up on the roof merely to get a breath of air, look around the city and smoke a cigarette. Simple as that. I was leaning on the parapet looking down at cars and trucks and at the traffic lights changing, people crossing the street—I knew the clothes were hanging on the line but didn't give it a thought—well, no, wondered when I first saw them why they were still on the line at night. The traffic stopped, that's when I heard the clothes flapping. Turned my head, cigarette smoke got into my eye. Three colored silk slips, stockings, two brassieres clipped in the middle of the rope—but they're gone now. Off the roof and down into the street. Can still see how the wind caught them and threw them around, which reminds me of something from many years ago although can't think what. Maybe a kite falling when the wind stopped—the cloth tail weaving, don't know for sure.

Have a feeling she's the one who stays up late. Have noticed a light burning on the 6th until very late. If that's the one it's possible she's going up to the roof sometime tonight to get her clothes. I could go up again and wait around. We might get acquainted. I've met her a few times looking through the mail on the table downstairs so there's no reason it would be strange to meet on the roof.

Waited almost 2 hours but no luck. Maybe I ought to take a few other things, it's all probably still scattered in the street. However somebody could see me collecting it, so don't think I will. Satisfied with what I've got. The texture's queer, coarse material. I wish I'd taken it before the smell of her body was washed out. Now it smells of the city wind.

Bianca must be awake, footsteps in the hall.

MAY 24

If I was a man what I'd do is beat her until she couldn't even scream—Christ why can't she let me alone!

Not interfering with her life so what does she want of me!
Just how much longer is she going to treat me like a child?
Let me alone! Do you hear?

Well, there I go again and ought to know better. The
thing is that men of intense perception such as myself must
learn to put up with these things, it's the penalty we pay for
our superiority. But there are certain occasions—no, don't
think about it Earl. Wouldn't matter what I told her, she'd
shake her head, look bored, lips tight as a purse. She
wouldn't believe it if I told her what I've done. Doesn't believe I'm capable of anything, thinks I do nothing except
talk about my plans. Not that she ever listens to them! Seldom listens to anything I say. I'd like to stuff her face full.
Reminds me of that pamphlet McA brought to work a few
weeks ago. Pictures of those devices—ropes, wheels, claws,
bridles, etc. I wonder how she'd like those! I wonder how
she'd like to be trussed and hoisted off the floor. I'd go after
her like a torpedo, after which there'd be little question as to
who is in control. I guess she'd respect me from then on.

Have tried praying, it doesn't help. My knees hurt & the
words break between my teeth like eggshells. What's going
to become of me?

Well, well, I see that police have arrested a suspect in the case of Lori Lengfeldt murder. Sausalito electri-
cian's assistant named Peter Brandt. They found her school
notebook in his car, plus other evidence they're keeping secret. Judging from the picture I'd say they bagged the right
bird—private pleasures always leave a trace & his face
shows it. I'd make a guess he was waiting to be caught, expecting it, halfway eager. How pretty he is with his wavy
blond hair and feminine lips. So in a few months it's the gas

119

chamber for Mr. Brandt. Public is in the usual snit, everybody wants personally to lynch him. What I'd like to do is
go out and piss in the middle of the street, it'll do as much
good as lynching Brandt. Yes. Why not? Later tonight indulge myself for once.

Now what other news this breezy Saturday? Convicts
stabbing each other at San Quentin but that's not unusual,
have lost track of how many this year. What else? High Society divorce, front-page news! She gets all the property because he was rude to her in front of guests. He missed his
chance, ought to have tied her to the bed, let her suffer for a
while, then leave his property to a mound of bloody flesh.

Hmm, let's see. Not much more that's interesting. Dog &
cat show at the auditorium. Also, some poet up on Green
Street sentenced to 30 days for using bad language. Government developed a new type of weapon for use against tanks
& armored cars. Getting ready for another war. It's about
time. Hurrah! Also—m-m-m—vandals in a cemetery toppling gravestones. What a shabby circus, and nobody can
convince me it isn't going to get worse.

MAY 26

Correct again, Earl Summerfield! Body of an old
man discovered this A.M. stuffed behind a big trunk in his
apartment on Haight Street. The cigarbox where he kept his
money is missing. Apartment spattered with blood, furniture overturned. Have clipped his picture for my scrapbook,
along with that of a grocery clerk at the Safeway store in
Belmont who blew his brains out yesterday afternoon. The
velvet ribbon of violence ties us all together. Destroy.
Blood of the slain. Fat of the mighty. If we keep this up
pretty soon there aren't going to be very many of us left.

MAY

My head beginning to feel as round & smooth as a glass bulb.

MAY 27

Thirteen employees at Bayview Hospital for Mentally Retarded have been arrested. Named in warrants: R. L. Hansen for beating child's head against the floor of a shower. Eloise Markup for striking an elderly patient's face with a knotted rope. Frederik Ramsey for breaking the jaw of one patient and throwing cup of hot cereal at another. Vince Bowen for hitting a baby with his fist and breaking the arm of a ten-year-old girl. Janice Toler for three counts of beating a young boy unconscious after tying him to a pillar, also beating heads of two patients against a wall. Evelyn Briffault, whipping. Annette Goodrich and Sidney Yeats, joint charges of whipping. Harold Cross on eight counts of dragging elderly patients into closets and kicking them into unconsciousness. Donald Pepp for two charges of whipping and beating. Selma Fisk, five counts, kicking & beating, also fracturing skull of one boy by throwing him against a bedpost. Jerold Thompson, three charges, hitting female patients with a boot. Hedda Kunitz, beating elderly males. There it is. I'm not surprised, not a bit. Destruction and Revenge. Corruption. Seed germinates in the earth, fertilizes, reproduces itself. That's how it's always going to be. Subtle forces impel us toward violent acts. I doubt if we're responsible. The truth of the matter must be that we have as little control over what we do as we have over the shape of our features.

Wondering what Bianca would think if she knew I was ready to beat somebody's head against a wall. Last thing on earth she expects.

121

MAY 28

I should be cautious about getting involved. Every person for himself. Expect no help from others, offer none. Limit yourself to expressions of sympathy. Fensdeicke for example—sick again but there's nothing I can do about it, nothing that I want to do. I don't want her to touch me. Mistrust that handkerchief, which may be dripping germs. Nor would it be a good idea to let Vladimir get too close, not with his Bolshevik ideas. Have no intention of exposing myself. No, I don't want our government putting me on file for being conspicuously friendly with him. That would be foolish. Suspicion equals collapse. My position here is too important to be risked. McA says the FBI is after him, claims 2 agents went in to talk to Mr. Foxx one day last month. I didn't see them but McA says they're unmistakable. Thinks V might be a Commie. Well, he looks the part with those long brown teeth & tobacco stains on his fingertips, so who knows. A relief I'm not foreign-born, apparently it makes quite a difference. Imagine the scandal if Vladimir should be deported! What a shock. No business of mine, but what I'll do is restrain myself, try to avoid sitting next to him at lunch, etc. Just now remembered Clegg's active in the Legion. I wonder if that could be significant. Did Clegg get in touch with the FBI? Sounds like an old movie plot but these days that's exactly how we live. Who'd believe the things we read in the paper every night? I certainly wouldn't. In fact I think there's somebody on the second floor of the Bureau watching us through a peephole—have often felt eyes on my neck. There could be a hole bored in the ceiling somewhere among the light fixtures. Telephones are being tapped, private conversations recorded, all of us taking notes on one another. Well, I'll stay out of trouble, avoid awkward situations.

Police car screaming down the street—I interpret that as a warning. Now there's a light in the apartment across the alley. Shades pulled down, people moving rhythmically back and forth as though dancing! Shadows of life. What's going on? What's going on?

MAY 29

McA suggested a movie after work. Strange idea, I thought, going to a show at 5 P.M., but then suddenly I knew what he had in mind. I guess I shouldn't have been surprised, women are all he thinks about. Lied clumsily saying Bianca and I were invited out tonight so I had to come home. He just grinned and shrugged. I wanted to go with him yet I didn't want to. That's a feeling I've known often enough. Where did he go? One of those places along Market Street, or else to some private club. Dirty fruit of abomination. Things on the floor. Tobacco and pee, rancid seats. Filth. Sewage. Men gliding along the aisles like shadows on the film. What goes on while they're pretending to watch? What pleasure does McA get from it? And what sort of women let themselves be photographed? I can imagine. If I was running things I'd chain them all together and spit on them, smear grease on those fat pink winking bellies. Tumtetum! I don't know why people degrade themselves. I don't know whether McAuliffe or the women disgust me more. Maybe I should have gone with him just to see the stinking truth. I could in fact go tomorrow, by myself. No need to be recognized. Wear a cap and jacket with collar turned up, buy the ticket and be inside before anybody noticed. I don't want to. The thought of it sickens me. I'd like to get in there and throw something at the screen. No doubt the police are paid to ignore those places. Yes, we're corrupt but who cares? Am I the only one? Well, they say it was what Luther discovered in Rome that first set him to thinking about his great revolt. He realized that Human Nature was a sink and he decided to scour it. That's worth considering.

MAY 30

Eleanor Highet, age 28, discovered in the garage of a Sutter Street apartment building just twelve and a half blocks from here, sliced from neck to pubes clean as a fish on a block. That was a quick one, in & out, nobody heard a thing, not a single screech. That's what she got for running around at night, the language of emotion leaves small room for doubt. Life more sacred during the Dark Ages.

MAY 31

Have put a hair in the diary every night for several weeks, so far it hasn't been disturbed—not that I thought it would be, but I'm shrewd enough to take certain precautions. B's puzzled, I'm aware of that. I know she slips up to the door and listens. Last week sometime—no, week before—came marching up to it, rattled the knob. "Earl, for God's Sake! What ARE you doing in there?" I don't meddle in her affairs, so it seems reasonable that she ought to leave me alone. Will point this out to her, point out I never say a word about her dates with Spach even though I know what she's up to—using him in order to satisfy her ambition. Well, it's all right with me if she wants to do that. I don't care what she does. She has her life, I have mine. Don't think she's really interested in anything I do, but she feels

124

obliged to ask. Doubt if she cares enough to snoop but I could be wrong. I don't underestimate the lioness so I ought to consider a new hiding place. No man wants the deep purposes of his soul held up to study.

JUNE 1

Midafternoon, bright & warm. I hear Bianca and her schoolgirls gabbling—absorbed by the problem of Final Examinations! How ludicrous. Let them fail, let them succeed, they have my blessing, I'm totally at ease. I am weighted and counterweighted as delicately as a scale. I'm able to stand erect with arms outstretched whenever it pleases me to do so. If I decided to soar out of here and soar along the corridor and glide into the room where they are—and out again and out of a window and soar over the top of the city—ah, what does it matter? What does anything matter? I won't argue with her again, no matter what she says, no matter how she debases me. It gives her pleasure to see me groveling, not merely because I am the Husband, but because I'm the man.

Suffering and confusion—all is past. I consider myself renewed, if not reborn. Especially gratifying is the fact that I no longer feel despondent. I'm now able to see the error of my past. I expected to live wretchedly & to suffer, therefore it became inevitable. Out of Nothing cometh nothing. It's as though I've heard the reproach of Moab, reviling of the children of Ammon.

Moab shall be as Sodom and the children of Ammon as

126

Gomorrah, even to the breeding of nettles. Saltpits & perpetual desolation.

JUNE 2

Sunday. Whore of Babylon is in the paper again today. Mara St. Johns considered one of twelve outstanding young people in the city. Finishing her third year at the university where she's an honor student. Secretary-treasurer of Students Civic Council. Zend Avesta Literary Society. Queen of Washington Birthday pageant in Aquatic Park. Active member of Cabrillo Charities. Unity Presbyterian choir. Lives with her mother in Pacific Heights—as if I didn't know! Father was an Army colonel killed during the last war. Also says she's been to Hollywood recently for a screen test—well! well! As if any more proof was needed about what she really is! However, what interests me most is that now she's teaching Thursday-night Bible class in the church basement. I might attend. Might get to my feet while she's speaking & accuse her of being exactly what I know she is. I wonder what people would think of me if I did That! Everybody's guessed the truth about her, why are they afraid to say so? And she knows what a slut she is. Remember the expression on her face when she looked at me. Won't ever forget. Should have jerked her down off the platform & then pointed to her, not saying a word. Too late, but what I can do is drop a little note to the pastor of that church, demand that he get rid of her. As Ye sow, so shall Ye reap.

10:45 P.M. Heigh ho, Earl. What to do now? Not sleepy and don't have to get up tomorrow.

THE DIARY OF A RAPIST

JUNE 3

First day of my vacation. I should have planned some activities. As it is I mostly sat around wondering how things were going at the Bureau. Tempted to drop by and say hello. Would be interesting to see how everything looks from the other side of the counter.

JUNE 4

Slept till 2:30 this afternoon, could hardly get out of bed I felt so stupefied. I'll be glad when vacation's over. Have felt tired ever since getting up. Bored by TV. Looked at cartoons in magazines, nibbled a bag of popcorn. How tiresome. Tweedle-de-dee.

Think of something to do—can't go another 12 days like this. I'm almost too tired to write, it's an effort to note these lines but so far this year I haven't forgotten a single day. I guess that's actually what keeps me going—my sense of discipline.

JUNE 5

Finally managed to get out of the apartment! Saw the exhibit of Dali paintings. Celestial crucifixion, Last Supper, etc., but I feel sure he's irreverent. Gilded buttocks, eggs & crutches, also a foetus on a fish hook. People without mouths. Then that woman on the balcony leaning forward with the rhinoceros horn behind her. So innocent. I was ready to give it a slash & would have, I suppose, if I had my way. Imagining or not that guard watching me? Every time

128

I looked at him he was staring my direction. Black hair growing out of his ears. What business is it of his what I do? He thinks he's important with his green uniform. Drifting around behind me wherever I went. Did I touch anything? All right, Earl, admit the truth, yes, a scratch to prove I'd been there.

After that? Along Pacific Heights, downhill to the Marina & sat on a bench for an hour or so watching ships coast under the bridge. Thought about experiences I've had, also reflected on things I should have done but was afraid to do. It's apparent I'm not getting much out of my life. But of course on the other hand I ought to consider myself extremely fortunate what with no serious financial problems, secure job, etc. For example, there I was enjoying my freedom in sight of those prisoners on Alcatraz. Were any of them looking across the water at me? What were they thinking? Probably that they'd give anything to be where I was. Yes, they were envious, as well they might be! In fact there must be a great number of people who'd like nothing better than to trade places with Earl Summerfield!

Now about tomorrow. I might suggest to Bianca that we go to the beach—it'll be warm enough unless the fog rolls in. Oh but already I can hear what she'd say. "Earl for the love of God! Can't you see I'm busy!" But if she wanted to go to the beach with me she could arrange it, the real reason is that she's ashamed to be seen in public with me. I'm not important enough. What does she expect me to be? She knew where I was working, knew my ambition was to climb steadily up through the ranks just like everybody else, but now for some reason that isn't good enough. Well, she overestimates herself. Ambitious, greedy—and it's beginning to show in her eyes, also her hands are changing shape. A few years from now I won't be able to look at her. I feel cheated. She lied to me. She's taken everything away—the breath out of my lungs. There are times when I believe she's actually draining my blood, substituting a sugary colorless liquid. Suppose I invited her to stroll across the Golden Gate Bridge & pushed her over the side when she stopped to light a cigarette. Dreamed about it one night. She went down with her red hair streaming. Say the hour was right, when the tide was strong, they'd never find the body. One shriek, then she'd be out of my life. I could be what I was meant to be, what I was born to be, not what I've become. Yes, and what's That? What HAVE you become Earl Summerfield? Since she usurped your place what do you think of yourself?

How did it start? I've taken her clothing off the hanger & examined it. I've opened drawers where her stuff is. I've felt the straps and the buttons but still I don't really understand. She appears to be what she is, but she's not, no more than I'm what everybody on earth takes me for. The fact is, she reminds me of Vladimir—smoking the way she does, her fingertips yellowing and her teeth getting stained. I've watched her reading with one eye closed against the smoke —he does that too. But I guess if there's any single thing it's that now she's got the breath of a man.

JUNE 6

Had planned to go to Unity Presbyterian tonight but it's still raining & besides I'm paralyzed. Lack the Will to go. Have difficulty doing anything, am so fatigued. Eyelids droop, listen to the splashing water. B's gone out to visit a friend but I've forgotten who. I don't care. So listless that I feel sick. What's going to become of me? Glad when life's over.

JUNE 7

Friday & the end of a week that might as well never have been. Wonder how things are going at the office. Ho hum.

Went to the zoo this afternoon. Asked Bianca if she wanted me to get anything on my way back but she just let me stand around waiting for an answer. Then "Earl for goodness sake!—if you're going all you need do is open the door!" That was my reward. Stared awhile at the back of her head—just stood and stared at the curlers in her hair but she wasn't concerned. She could wash it when I'm not home but she knows how I hate the smell of that soap she uses, also that sour rinse or vinegar, whatever it is. She knows I don't like it, which is why she does it. Does everything she can think of to let me know I'm nothing in her life. I'm starting to feel like an X-ray picture. Blurred bones, gray flesh. One black spot in the picture—my wedding ring. Well, no point arguing with her so I went out & shut the door softly, then peeped through the mail slot but didn't see much. She kept on sitting in that chair but she knew I was watching, I could tell somehow. Also the lid of the slot squeaks. However it might do her some good, let her know I'm aware of what's going on.

Frankly don't care for the zoo, except of course I do like leopards. Also the birds. Avoided the pens of elephants, etc. on account of their stink. Watched our little cousins on that painted concrete island for a while, then rode to Spreckels Lake & home again. Bored.

Midnight. Light rain falling. A few minutes ago a gull settled on the telephone post, folded his wings & simply sat there gazing this direction. He knew I was here behind the glass. Couldn't guess what he wanted, but something. He

131

turned around after settling, opened his beak and spoke, then flew across to the window ledge & gobbled up a snail. How did the snail get there? Noticed her at the last moment —dragging herself along by the tongue through the rainy lamplight. Naked and vulnerable. Countless mysteries of Nature.

JUNE 8

Saturday. Still depressed. B was out and I did not know what to do with myself so I painted the bathroom, but should have asked permission—the lioness is enraged. I've wasted money, she could have got paint at a discount, why didn't I tell her what I was going to do, etc. And of course I got the wrong color. I'm at fault. So far as she's concerned life is THIS or THAT. I should have told her the actual reason I decided to paint that room was to get rid of her odor. Ointment, cosmetics, sprays—yes, and the hair she leaves in the bowl. Every time I go in there I think about her eternal biologic Functioning. Bags & containers, tissue, powder, combs—always the smell of putrefaction. A slimy trail. Thought fresh paint would make it more pleasant but she blamed me. What have I done wrong? Besides, I enjoyed the work. Very refeshing. I'm not suited for this sedentary life, ought to work more often with my hands. Envy laborers. Maybe I should have been a carpenter. No matter what—anything better than this. Swallow prepared foods, observed closely as a bug. What sort of life is this? Feel as though I'm held by invisible leather straps. If only I could get away. I think of coral islands in the South Pacific. If I was there I could lie down to sleep at night without inhaling stale talcum. I could go to sleep on a sandy beach with stars overhead. Drink the milk of coconuts. Fish. Swim naked, fearlessly among sharks. That's the sort of life I should be leading. Instead, what? Earl Summerfield lives in a shabby apartment in foggy San Francisco. Day after day surrounded by thousands of slushy leaking bodies smeared with ungents and rouge. Elaborate garden snails.

Now 3 in the morning, almost. I shut my eyes but have no desire to sleep. Self-fulfillment seems pretty remote.

JUNE 9

Bianca and I to Golden Gate Park! Our first afternoon "together" since? Impossible to say. We behaved like new lovers, hand in hand. I do love my wife. How wonderful to believe that I still love her. She's modest and truthful, whatever her faults. They say that the more of love you know, the greater must be your sorrow. On the other hand, if you withhold yourself from love you will find yourself free from pain. This is so because all earthly things and Love itself must end with pain. That's the end of love. Sadness is the end of joy. Revulsion the last full note of pleasure. Dead too soon is happiness. Dead too soon.

JUNE 10

Monday. I don't feel like writing. Optimism of yesterday gone up in a puff of smoke. When will I learn to be realistic? Quit overestimating people because it's always the same. Not just B. Everybody. There's no love, only hate. For example, headline today—Icepick Murder! That's what we love. See it everywhere. Death and destruction. I'm not responsible & am sick of being Concerned. From now on I think I'll just observe whatever happens without worrying over it. Withdraw from the world like some artist painting a religious scene.

133

JUNE 11

Tuesday & it occurs to me that next week I'll be back at work. Vacation scoots past quick as a bus. I'm not enjoying it, just been shoveling time, mostly thinking about everybody at the office & trying not to fall asleep. Had an exciting evening, however. To the boxing matches at Kezar Stadium. Got up and yelled and waved my arms along with the others. It's an unusual sensation—belonging to a crowd, contributing your little bit to that blind Emotion.

Humdedum—sit in one chair after another, avoiding Bianca as much as anything, that's what my vacation consists of. Watch television & contemplate the vacancy of existence. Have a feeling B is disillusioned, but so am I. Nothing either of us can do about that. No sense worrying. Speak my name aloud & listen to the echo. Clip my fingernails, search the Chronicle for items of interest. What a vacation. If I'd just been able to make up my mind about what to do, could have gone to Santa Cruz, gone water skiing. At least a few days would help. Monterey. Carmel. Visit those rich men's country clubs, act like I belonged and was just looking around. Maybe I could have gotten in a game of golf, been acquainted with them by this time. Instead I just sat around.

Went through the Chronicle again. Reread that article about schoolgirls carrying razors in their beehive hair or folded into their brassieres. At first it's astonishing but now not so much, not while our own government's threatening to kill half the people on earth. Tit for Tat. Much stamping of feet. I'd like to call attention to what's going on, but who am I? Who'd listen to anything I had to say? Earl Summerfield? Who? I know what I am. Yes, I'll be in the Chronicle someday—a few lines on the 8th page. Unidentified man jumped off the Gate Bridge, worked for the Department of

Employment, leaves a wife, no children, no explanation given. Well, Earl, there's a little joke without realizing it— Unidentified but then you mention you had a wife, job, no children.
Bored. Sweet God how bored I am. Feel like a ball of string.
Better now after a nap. In fact, quite alert. Indolence capable of energy. I don't know why I was suddenly overcome by that desire to sleep. Anyway, now it's quiet outside, must be very late. Trash collectors banging cans around farther up the street. Just now put my head out the window and could hear their voices. Truck's grinding along in this direction. Think I'll put on my jacket and take a walk. Might make a telephone call—wake up Miss St. Johns, ask if she carries a razor.

JUNE 12

Austin Lee Travis, Negro, age 39, executed this morning at one minute after ten in the famous Green Room, room of the apple-green walls. He choked and coughed and gagged for nearly six minutes after the gas reached his nostrils and wasn't officially pronounced dead until eleven after the hour. He put up a stronger fight than most, screamed, wagged his head, held his breath, etc. Made quite a fuss. Apparently didn't think they should kill him. One witness says Travis almost broke the straps holding him in the chair. That certainly would have made a show. He tears one hand loose, then manages to break the other straps, staggers to his feet and tries to open the door but the handle's outside. Beats on it while the gas boils around him. Kicks it—gaping, drooling. Witnesses, guards & executioner helpless— not able to do a thing. Victim didn't Submit. They thought he would but oh no he had a different idea—decided not to

135

behave as he was supposed to. Panic! Nobody brave enough to open the door. Stand there watching, everybody hopes he'll die & solve the problem. Yes indeed, that would be a spectacle worth seeing. Suppose he actually got out of the chamber, then what? Staggering around the room vomiting poison on the witnesses, rolling on the floor gagging and coughing and begging somebody to help. Mmm—guess sooner or later they'd have to call for a stretcher or one of those little carts and wheel him away to the hospital to try and save his life even though they'd just been trying to kill him. Afterward, if he recovered, what would happen? Embarrassing. What to do? Couldn't let him go. I guess they'd be forced to lock him up again, set a new date, try once more. Well, it's a pity he's dead. I wish he'd gotten loose long enough to let us smell ourselves.

JUNE 13

Am feeling excited. Went this evening to Unity Presbyterian and no sooner got off the bus than I saw M. St. J. driving into the alley behind the church. In the basement door she went, left her ritzy car unlocked just as though there was nobody else in the world! All by herself!— doesn't believe there are other people! Nobody's good enough for her, that's what she thinks! At least a streetwalker's honest, not this filthy slut. I suppose her mother's worse. High-class tramps is what they are, mother and daughter working as whores at a fancy Vallejo Street address. That's what I believe. Why else would her mother let her get up on a stage in front of everybody? There can't be any other reason. But the Time will come. Vengeance is mine, saith the Lord.

JUNE 14

Still thinking about her slimy invitation last February. But I returned the compliment—left my own Calling Card and wonder what she thought about That! Probably decide it was an accident & won't happen again. Yes, that's what she'll think, it's accidental. Coincidence. How stupid she is. Get somebody to wash the seat—the fiancee, of course. She'll ask him to clean it up. He'll do it & she knows it, that's why she'll make him do it. Must say I get more than a little satisfaction thinking about him cleaning up after me.

Restless & ill at ease. Just now examined my teeth in the mirror and tried to smell my breath. Suppose it's time for a visit to the dentist. Ought to go more often. Keeping my lips together when I smile because of that chipped tooth. He could fix it. No reason for me to be ashamed to ask. Embarrassed about vanity, which is one of my great faults.

Well, the sun's finally going down. Fix myself a bite to eat before long. B's note says she won't be home till late. I guess she's doing something for that Republican organization again, seem to remember she said something about it a few days ago.

Can't calm down. Had better not go out tonight or there could be Trouble. Keep inside where it's safe. I wish she'd lock me in.

Head's beginning to swell up like a loaf of bread. Feel like I'm flying around in some fantastic world full of those old winged gods—Babylonian, Greek, etc.

JUNE 15

Last night laced myself into one of Bianca's girdles, then put on stockings, hat with a veil, and paraded before the mirror. No wonder they get so arrogant. Flesh, hair, perfume & flimsy rags. Saw my shadow on the wall and thought the whore of Babylon was in the room. Opened the window to relieve myself, afterward very tired, numb, disappointed. Can't get used to what I am. Don't want to be this way but what else is there?

JUNE 16

Sickened whenever I think about self-indulgence. During the Middle Ages they say the monks occasionally used to murder their abbot for preaching to them about better behavior. Nobody can preach to me, only myself, and I suppose it remains to be seen whether I can change or whether Abbot Summerfield's going to get a knife in the ribs.

Tomorrow's Monday once again. Vacation ended.

JUNE 17

It was just the same as if I'd never been away. Nobody particularly glad to see me, on the other hand nobody Minded that I'd returned. Indifference. Total indifference. Out of courtesy a few asked where I went—somehow a rumor got started that I'd flown to Hawaii. Said I'd decided simply to relax in the city puttering about, and that satisfied them. So the whole thing's resumed, but maybe I should say it starts again. Say I'll start again, all over, adjust to life as it is, not as I want it to be. For instance, now I can see I didn't deserve a promotion—it was presumptuous of me because really I wasn't qualified to become a supervisor. All right, now I've admitted this the thing to do is to apply myself to the work, make absolutely no mistakes—none!

—meanwhile treat everybody formally, make plans for the future. I'm still young. Next year I'll be in line for a promotion, it's simply a matter of time until they recognize me. I think I'll incline my head to the supervisors when I enter & leave. A suggestion of dignity. Yes, they won't fail to notice it. Truly important people always are dignified. I believe that's the key to my success. I'll pay more attention to the fine detail of life, examine the pattern of existence, make myself clearer & clearer until at last everything Fits. Then nothing in the world can come between me and the pattern.

JUNE 18

Spent most of the day thinking and have decided that our pattern is Monochromic. The evidence can't be ignored, it's apparent everywhere. Particularly impressed by Aneurine's tone of voice, also the way she has of washing her hands together while talking. It does become clear, yes, one needs to observe & listen, to smell and Sense with senses too delicate for apprehension until the object itself has begun to speak. Then, but only then, are we able to understand.

So concludes this Tuesday & a profitable Tuesday it was! I feel expansive and tolerant.

JUNE 19

People in the office are signaling. I've noticed on two occasions since Monday that Fensdeicke stroked her desk while looking at McAuliffe. Immediately afterward she glanced in my direction. It's obvious that they've been talking about me. My guess is that they're beginning to realize the Injustice. Another interesting point is whether or not

Foxx has been in on these discussions. If so he might have forwarded the material about me to Sacramento. I'm very curious, I won't pretend I'm not. Keep an eye on things. Continue as I am. Patience finally will be rewarded.

Would it be a good idea to grow a mustache? Certainly would add power to my features. Lips are fleshy and jaw recedes—have never been quite satisfied with the bottom half of my face in contrast to the eyes which are very alert and intelligent. Not flattering myself. The truth, as always. One of my good points. But a mustache might give Fensdeicke and Aneurine the impression I was trying to assert myself, emphasizing my presence. No, better to let them recognize superiority without attracting attention. On the other hand—I don't know, don't know! Don't know what to do.

Moon's rising, still here I sit! So many hours wasted.

JUNE 20

Thursday night, just got back. Started a few minutes earlier than last week. Waited across the street to see what I could see and into the alley she went just as though pulled on a string. Or maybe she knows I'm watching. Hadn't thought of that! If that's the case what does she want? What does she want me to do? Does she want me to climb into the back seat of the car and wait till the lecture is over? Then what? Cut her apart like a cabbage, simple enough. Does she think the hand of God is going to reach down past the steeple to save her? I guess she thinks so but I have a different opinion. Justice is Justice. Such a lady. Oh yes! What does she do in the basement? Hadn't thought of That either! What goes on down there when they say there's a Bible class? I can guess, don't need to be told. I can see it all. I know what's going on, am not exactly blind. Next

140

week go up to her & say I know all about it. Or perhaps not a word, merely point at It, then calmly walk away. They say there's putrefaction at the heart of the lily & the ewe lamb shall be gored.

JUNE 21

Mr. Foxx sent for me this afternoon but I don't know why. It was certainly a curious "interview." I got quite excited when Mrs. Fensdeicke came over to me and said that I should report to his office. I looked at her very stupidly and exclaimed, "Now?" She nodded, slipped away without saying another word. The news made me dizzy. Sugarplum!—it popped into my head, meaning Promotion! I hardly remember getting off my stool. McAuliffe glanced across and winked at me, as though he knew what it meant. Vladimir peered at me through his glasses. Clegg didn't notice, although I must have looked as pale as ashes. I kept saying to myself: They haven't forgotten me! They haven't forgotten me! And Mr. Foxx stood up when I entered his office, shook hands and offered me a seat. Anybody would have thought we were equals. I was afraid to speak, I had no idea what I'd say. Some awful word might have popped out, something I didn't mean. But he was all questions. Questions! Questions! Was I dissatisfied with my job? Did I feel that Miss Aneurine was a competent supervisor? Did I expect to make the Bureau my life work? Would I care for a cigarette? Accepted the cigarette as a matter of courtesy & told him I would smoke it after work. I believe he was testing my sense of discipline. If so, he ought to be reassured. I'm not altogether pleased with myself, but I do take pride in certain of my characteristics. He didn't mention Sacramento although I'm positive the folder on his desk concerned me. They must have sent him additional information. Yes, that's

141

what it was. I wish he'd told me but the Bureau's conservative and with reason, otherwise the office would be choked with rumor. No doubt I'll be hearing soon—within a few days. I should try to behave as though nothing's going to happen but I'm excited, doubly excited because it's puzzling.

So ends this week & I scarcely can wait until Monday.

JUNE 22

Didn't go for my customary walk this evening, have had too much to think about. After supper I locked the door, told B I didn't wish to be disturbed. She laughed. No matter what I say she twists it about in order to make me ridiculous. Tonight my dinner's served on a paper plate. An ordinary paper plate. I stared at it until she got the point. It makes no difference to her. "Earl I have no intention of ruining my hands washing dishes. Now eat your supper." I was about to spit on the food, could feel my head closing up like a fist. The reason she serves my food on paper is so that she can have more time to herself. Now it's real estate. I think she's planning to borrow from the bank to buy a piece of ground in the hills behind Mill Valley. Hold it like a spider until somebody else wants it. I have an urge to buy a package of paper plates, tie them with a ribbon and present them to her as an expression of contempt.

Thinking of what she's done to me. Also what others have done. Thinking about that time last April I wanted to make love and my own wife lay on the bed biting her lip. She didn't know how close she was to Death. But I suppose millions marry for love without love ever revealing itself to them. I guess I'm no worse off than a lot of others.

JUNE 23

Maybe the trouble is that I love myself too much —the fact that I'm Earl Summerfield. Is it that simple? Can anybody love himself like that? Well, I don't know, it seems to me nothing else is as important. Earl Summerfield. Earl Summerfield. For one thing it's an unusual name & suits me. At the Bureau, for example, or on the street, elsewhere, people glancing toward me with definite respect—yes, I've been aware of it but have taken care not to acknowledge their looks. They wouldn't be staring at me unless they recognized me. It wouldn't be dignified to return the stares.

How quiet this room is. Well!—must have forgotten to wind the clock, it stopped just now. That's the reason for the silence. Frightened me at first. Then that dog howling across the street. If he keeps it up there's going to be one less mutt in our neighborhood. Powdered glass in meat would teach him a thing or two.

JUNE 24

Disappointment at the office—Mr. Foxx was away, which explains why there wasn't any word about my new position. Perhaps tomorrow. All weekend I looked forward to this Monday. Hardly turned out as I expected. McAuliffe at lunch telling us about his weekend at Stinson Beach with some little tramp. Nobody wanted to hear the details but of course that didn't stop him. Filthy. Vulgar. Always dirt under his fingernails, whiskey on his breath. And has he paid me back? Oh no. I ought to threaten him somehow, but I don't guess even that would have too much effect on him. He's a deadbeat, a cheat, liar, without any

143

respect for anybody. But of course he's not much different from the majority.

Well, I'm quite fortunate. Whether anybody recognizes it or not I'm markedly superior to most people. I have a sense of morality. Most don't. They take advantage of others but I never do. I have weaknesses enough, of course, and nobody is quicker to admit them. For one thing I'm obsequious, practically unctuous, so that I give the impression that I'm not even aware of how others are Using me. Then, too, don't want to offend anybody. Cowardice. Yes, I've always been cowardly. I'm perfectly willing to admit this as well. Easily disturbed. The truth is I have the soul of a cocker spaniel, have no hesitation about rolling on my back in hopes people will treat me kindly. I'll lick anybody's boot. If there was any one thing about myself that I could change it would be That. I hate my cowardice. I'd like to say what I think, no matter what happens, but I never do. Have never been able to do it. Not able to challenge people. Avoid trouble. Afraid that something's about to happen. Exactly what, I've never known.

I'll have to get along under these circumstances. Here I am, Earl Summerfield, created as I am & all I dare hope for is to be reconciled with my miserable deficiencies.

JUNE 25

Tuesday. Mr. Foxx still away. F said he's in Sacramento for a conference. Patience. Patience.

What's new? Not much. Surprises nobody our district attorney has announced he's going to ask the death penalty for Peter Brandt in Lengfeldt case. Evidence conclusive. Her notebook in his car, one of her bracelets discovered in his house. Also, D.A. said he'll produce witnesses placing Brandt near the school that afternoon. More needed, or is that already enough? At any rate it's no concern of mine whether Brandt goes free or performs the Dance of Death.

Fee-fi-fo-fum, my blood feels thick, must be the full moon. I'm greasy as a goat, choked with fluids halfway up my throat. I'll pop into a house tonight—it's that or unburden myself some other way, not that I have much choice.

JUNE 26

Somewhere on 4th Avenue, I think. Green stucco duplex with a bicycle in the back yard, sandbox, tire hanging by a rope from the limb of a tree. The garage was unlocked, and I remember there was a cheap camera lying on the front seat of the car, also the hood was up so he must have been tinkering with the motor. Garden shears and gloves on a shelf, flashlight, coil of red plastic hose, pile of newspapers, bottle of turpentine. Electric lawnmower parked beneath the stairs. Smelled of gas and fertilizer. Ran a splinter into my thumb feeling my way up the steps. Upper door was also unlocked. Everybody asleep. I could sense them on the second floor. Not a sound except the refrigerator humming, which I heard immediately. Went into the kitchen for a look because I had a feeling it was the same as ours, but not quite. They had a chicken wrapped in aluminum foil, leftovers from dinner, oranges, milk, etc. From there I walked into the breakfast room and stumbled against a chair. Was afraid the noise woke them up but it didn't, anyway nobody moving around upstairs. Umm—let's see. What was in the center hall? Big porcelain vase filled with artificial flowers. Magazines on the table, also some keys. A couple of letters ready to be mailed. One to a Los Angeles bank, other I think was to some people in San Diego. Put them in my pocket but then put them back on the table. Don't know what I had in mind. Let's see—can't remember

145

what I did next, suddenly was on hands and knees crawling across the rug looking for just the right spot. Afterwards went to sleep for a few minutes. Woke up with a loud gasp but have no idea what caused that except I must have dreamed. I think that did wake them upstairs, didn't wait to find out. Through the back door and across the fence quick as a cat.

How long until next time? I never know. It rises suddenly around me and I'm gone like a fish in a wave.

JUNE 27

Sick of myself, sick of Earl Summerfield, sick of the ideas that crawl into my head and cling to the inside of my skull. Might as well be a swarm of roaches. The problem is how to clean them out. I can't seem to. Tonight I didn't mean to do a thing, thought I'd have a pleasant walk possibly toward Pacific Heights because everything was warm & starry. Then all at once in the telephone booth. I think I took her by surprise. "Who's calling?" Maybe I should have dropped a hint. Well, I did of course, telling her I knew about the Bible class. The little whore. This is Earl Summerfield!—that's what I should have said. Do you hear me? Earl Summerfield! You better listen if you know what's good for you! Yes, that's how I should have spoken to her, then told her the truth about herself—as if she doesn't know! Certainly everybody ought to tell the truth. That would make the world a much more decent kind of place.

JUNE 28

Friday. Those 14-year-olds are going to be here tomorrow. When they go to the toilet I can put a chair in the

146

hall & see over the transom. Would like to get a look at that one with the birthmark.

Tum tum la tum tum—very nice tune on the radio. Sounds familiar but can't place it. Suppose I ought to go to bed but am feeling much too jolly.

B at the door again! Good thing she can't see what I'm doing—waving it like a flag at her—otherwise there'd be the Devil to pay. Yes, all right Bianca, I'm sorry I woke you up. TUM tum LA la tum. In a minute, Bianca, don't interrupt. Put it away, button up & hide the book.

JUNE 29

Popped out of the apartment this afternoon to hold the elevator for Robin and Twinka. What was my reward? "You dirty old bastard! You let us alone!"

They're going to pay for that—oh shit I'll make them pay —little tramps. They'll pay for this. They'll pay. I swear they'll pay. And my dear wife too.

JUNE 30

Sunday alone. Avoided B since yesterday. Hid. Spoke to nobody. People look small as though watching them through binoculars.

JULY 1

Next Thursday's the 4th of July and there's going to be a fancy celebration! Folk dancing in the afternoon, entertainment, popcorn, dogs, balloons, municipal band music, ice cream, Old Glory waving in the breeze. I might attend, it belongs as much to me as to anybody. Then in the evening a display of fireworks at the Marina green. Sky-rockets, Roman candles—gives me an idea.

Off to bed with you, Earl Summerfield! You've peered far enough into another's future.

JULY 2

Jesus said that if anybody comes to Him who doesn't hate his own father, mother, wife, children, brothers, sisters, as well as his own life also—such a person cannot ever hope to become His disciple.

JULY 3

Crown wickedness with a Turd.

148

JULY

JULY 4

JULY 5

White roots grow deep. The blossom is dark, the odor foul.

JULY 6

Midnight. One more day ended. I sit here listening for a knock at the door.

JULY 7

She's afraid to tell them, she'd feel exposed & cheap! Or do I overestimate the bitch? What does she think about me? Why did she stare at me?

JULY 8

Monday. Talk at the Bureau, yet not as much as I expected. I joined the discussion, it would look suspicious to say nothing. However I may have talked too much, people gazing at me strangely. Furthermore, once or twice I smiled. How explain that?—if somebody asked. From now on I'll stay alert and emphasize innocence by ignorance. Act the expected part.

149

JULY 9

Of course the advantage lies with me but still—well, the longer I worry the more I realize there's no answer to the questions I could raise. Not unless—not unless What? Not unless I exposed myself. Interesting to think about this. I try not to think of it but always the idea returns. What would happen to me? I know what happens to others, but that has nothing to do with me. It does, of course, but I can't imagine it.

Suppose I went back. Or I could telephone, give my name and address. Perhaps I'd mention where I work, identify some of the people there—what a scandal THAT would cause, to say the least! Mr. Foxx would have a hard time ignoring me after a thing like that. Years from now just the name Earl Summerfield would cause people to stop whatever they were doing. Earl Summerfield! Yes, I knew him. I could tell you a great deal about him—if I wanted to.

Foolish to consider. Go on as I have. Grain was sown in the heart of Adam. How much ungodliness it has produced up to this hour. And how much more until the day of Judgment.

JULY 10

Despondent this evening. Why should I care what becomes of me? Let others decide. Let others be concerned. Let them find me. Let them discover me—if they're able.

150

JULY 11

Who knows how our ideas come to us? From above, or below? From without, or within? Thoughts we never think. Those shears an inch from her throat, suddenly I felt a wish to marry her—I never dreamed that, God knows! I almost asked the slut. Would have, I think, but was afraid she'd start to laugh. Maybe she wouldn't laugh at me. I don't know. It's too late now, she hates me. Hates all men because of me. I didn't have any right to do what I did—it was wrong. But of course on the other hand it's what she deserved. She's a vile dirty little bitch. I should have ripped open her belly and snapped a picture of the mess—sent it to the Chronicle. Everybody ought to see exactly what she is. Exactly what she is. Everybody ought to see. That's right.

JULY 12

She'd point me out if she had the chance. Then who'd believe anything I tried to say? Who'd believe Earl Summerfield under those circumstances? Nobody. Not one person. If I said she joined me against the church wall, who'd listen? She joined me and that's true, but in front of others she'd act the professional Innocent—not saying anything, just pointing. That's how it would be. Oh yes! But just the same, how soon will she taunt another man?—that's what I'd like to know. I might call & ask.

Must admit to feeling garrulous this evening. Is it because I haven't been found out? Eight days! La la!—well, is freedom so important? Don't know, can't seem to come to any conclusions, nothing much matters. Eight days I guess I didn't actually expect. Don't know what I expected. But who's going to say I won't have eight more? After that— who knows!

Another hour gone. Feeling much subdued & poetic. Head full of beautiful ideas.

The Devil is supposed to have a forked penis so he can commit sodomy and fornication simultaneously, yet we build gods in the image of ourselves because it's implausible to do otherwise, consequently there's no reason for me to feel upset. How can one already worn out by this corrupt world understand Incorruption? Let the human race lament & let animals rejoice, etc. Yes, that's how it is, for the world has lost its youth and the times are beginning to grow old.

That's right, I've been right all along. I wasn't wrong. And after putting up with what I have—insults thrust into my head like sticks—well, the thought escaped. Skittered off crookedly as a butterfly. But I know what I'll do next Monday, offer a theory. Predict "he" won't be caught because he's intelligent. If anybody's interested I'll elaborate, mention examples, memorize a few statistics. Also I could remind them of how easily people forget, offer to place a bet that two months from now, or less, not one of them will be able to recall her name. Or I might bet that within one year not even the police will care.

Yes, all things fade like the memory of a stranger once seen in the street. Moments of love & violence, hours of bitterest hate. True. Of millions of words addressed to me how many could I repeat? Five hundred at the most. And the faces of women—the many faces that I've seen, how many would I recognize? Thirty or forty. What have they taught me? Nothing. I've listened to them talk & watched them wherever they go, but Magnus is going to find a lump of gold in the desert before a woman will teach me anything. Small humor, less wit, no philosophy, nothing but that dull resignation to Fate. Mercy & forgiveness. No matter what

we do they forgive us. How strange. Unlike the nature of a man.
Why is it they continue to love us when we treat them as we do? Nobody can be sure, there are false answers to every question.

JULY 13

Very late but I'm not sleepy. Might go for a walk downtown and look at posters in the windows of the travel bureaus. Or maybe just walk slowly through the streets of San Francisco breaking things till I'm stopped. I don't care. I'm free but it doesn't interest me. Maybe I'm free against my will. I guess I can choose.

How very different I feel tonight. Remembering for instance how quick and powerful I felt as soon as I touched her. Hadn't expected anything like that, but one touch and then I was capable of—oh, I suppose of just about anything. I couldn't do it now, but that night I was able to hear the slightest sound, and it wouldn't be much trouble to run away from anybody. Fog drifting over the top of the church, cold midsummer night. Suppose what I keep thinking about the most is that she didn't seem especially surprised. Well, of course she had warnings enough, that's probably the reason. Forgot how many times I telephoned, also there were the notes. Yes. But another puzzling thing is why she wanted me to talk. Say something! Say something! On her knees in the corner trying to see my face & begging me to talk. I don't know, think I did say something. Annoyed when she asked whether I believed in God. In times like these? God doesn't mean any more to us than a tinkling cowbell.

I've never felt quite the way I do just now. I don't know what to make of it. Not a sound within this room & I feel like asking questions but am uncertain what to ask.

153

Holding up both hands in front of my face & somehow had the impression they were covered with black seeds. Otherwise, no sensation. Not even when I think about her. Seems like everything's slowed down. Here it is already the 13th but time's dragging. Sand sifting gradually through the atmosphere. Maybe things are going on that I don't know much about. That's possible. Yes, that's possible.

JULY 14

Last night went back for a look at the church but didn't get too close, simply walked by as though on my way somewhere. Didn't see anybody, no sign of police, but I won't be fooled by that. Whatever I am, I'm not a fool. Let's see—then across the street and through that vacant lot looking for her shoe. Why did I keep one, throw away the other? Didn't want her to follow, I remember that's why I took them off her feet, but going through the lot for no good reason suddenly tossed one into the weeds. Well, I suppose I was afraid they'd be found if—no, that can't be it, all I can think of now is that I didn't want to give them up completely, so kept one. Now I want them both, they'd look nice together & might help somehow. Bring her that much closer. If I need—there's Bianca coughing again! Propped up in bed, no doubt, pillows behind her back and those horn-rim glasses with a rhinestone chain looped around her neck. Smoking, squinting through the smoke while she examines stock-market reports—I don't need to look, every night's the same. I never thought it would turn out like this. We've drawn back from each other. Avoiding each other like two little organisms under a microscope. Floating in separate worlds.

Well, sing softly Earl! The night of the soul is dark, twice as dark as the ocean floor.

154

JULY 15

Seem to be getting more & more confused, not attending to my work. Could be the weather, or possibly the news? In the office they stare at me—sure of it. Also, I think Bianca's been watching me. What's on her mind? Have I been—no, no, I haven't done a thing unusual. But it's hard to tell. And then of course we speak Inaudibly. We're talking even when our lips are shut.

Recently have felt extremely removed. Detached as though wandering around in a hall of mirrors. During supper caught myself gazing into her eyes at my own reflection. How odd that people can be so close, yet never touch. I'm sorry about that. I'm truly sorry for everything we've lost.

JULY 16

If I had one wish I'd wish to be a woman. And I'd go traveling by myself. Put on an attractive suit with a crisp white blouse, wear rings, necklaces and perfume. I'd travel to the places I've heard about, places I'll never see. There I'm sure I'd meet some important people. Artists and millionaires. What a life that would be! It's what I deserve. I'd never worry about how much a meal is going to cost or—ah well Earl, you're either lucky or you're not & it's as simple as that! You'll never see Bangkok so you might as well get used to it, find peace within yourself. You won't be leaving the office until they force you to quit because you don't know what else to do and don't have enough guts to try another sort of life. At least I can admit that to myself. And that my life's ruined. How long before somebody finds out? Then what? I won't think about it, I'll pay attention to my

155

work. Months could go by, maybe years. I might escape. In fact there's no reason to be alarmed, not if I control myself. As long as I can keep my job I think everything will be all right.

JULY 17

Foggy these past days which could be the reason I've hardly opened my mouth. But the fog's started to lift, wind from the north tonight & on the roof a few minutes ago I could see lights glittering across the bay.

JULY 18

Thursday midnight. Feeling about the same. Changing self's more difficult than I thought. How to pull away from the past? How does a beetle escape when one leg's fastened to a spiderweb? But I can do it and be reborn. Flesh is merely flesh. Begin a new life without moving from where I am, not even altering the letters of my name.

Fire engine—thought it was stopping here but has gone now, turned the corner. Gone except for the noise hanging inside my head. Also, I still see the flash of red light. Gongs and sirens—Earl Earl EARL! echoing in my skull. Why it is I don't know, but I seem to hear Aunt Ollie's voice & the screen door banging, summer twilight and something frying on the stove. Potatoes. I can smell them. What else? Sheet lightning beyond the school. Across the street Lucille skipping rope. That was July twenty years ago. Hmm. Who'd guess it would come to this? For some reason I feel very disappointed.

Head still aches. Might as well try to sleep.

JULY 19

The Bureau's tedious under any circumstances & seems more so now that V's on his vacation. He won't be back for another 7 days. Said he planned to spend most of his two weeks playing chess at the union hall down by the wharf. Seems to me like a waste of time but I guess he doesn't think so. Clegg goes off next. He and his wife planning to rent a trailer and take a leisurely trip to visit relatives in British Columbia. Well, I wouldn't be interested in that either but still I envy them—V and Clegg both. Easy satisfactions. Easy rest at night. They don't know what it means to be cruelly twisted. In fact, how many do?

JULY 20

Saturday. Again today and again tonight. Angered by the way I indulge myself. God knows I didn't choose my habits, something goes through me like an electric wire & there's nothing I can do. Can't prevent myself. Now I sit here covered with perspiration and hope for a knock at the door, hope somebody discovers. Hours turn, hours turn. Why can't they find me? Do I have to go out again? After that once more? How much longer? How much longer? How much longer?

JULY 21

No doubt in my mind about what I should have done when I had the chance. Knowing she's alive is what I hate. Knowing that as long as she lives I won't be able to forget. I thought that I had thought of everything but forgot what I should easily have remembered—that I couldn't forget. It's like a theme out of Purgatory, or dry agonies of early Christian fathers & no help. No help from anyone.

If only she'd resisted I'm not sure what—might have killed her, might have run away in a panic—but she obeyed, did everything I ordered. Beside the wall, kneeling there quiet as a pony with soft nipples hanging down. Somehow I thought about the Queen of Sheba when I saw that shag of hair—ought to have shaved it and kept it in a box. According to the Bible this woman came to prove Solomon "with hard questions" but when she had seen him in his glory there was no spirit left in her. That probably was how she felt. Yes, otherwise she would have screamed or fought against me.

Well, here I am yawning. Tik toc tik toc tik toc! I don't know how many hours I've been absorbed in thought. Soon I suppose it'll be growing light beyond the Berkeley hills.

JULY 22

No reason I can't visit her again. Why not? I'm free to do as I please, nobody on earth can prevent me. For the first time I know what Freedom is. Freedom that's absolute. I used to envy people I decided were important, from Mr. Foxx on up to famous scientists, explorers, millionaire bankers, etc., but now I look down on them. Not one of them compares with me. And furthermore—this building just swayed! It's quieted down now, guess it was a small earthquake.

Remembering how she moved beneath me. She did respond, it wasn't long until she did. Not long until the senses of the body overcame her mind. They can't resist us, not one of them. I'll never know exactly what it means, they live so

158

much inside themselves, tangled flowers fascinated by their own idleness. Plants in a greenhouse suffocating us. All of them, even the ugliest. Aneurine dragging that shriveled red leg & pausing to smile at me—it disgusts me so I can't feel pity. Why doesn't she leave me alone? If everybody would leave me alone I'd be all right.

Now about tomorrow, let's think. Doubt if we'll be particularly busy at the Bureau. In another sense "tomorrow" what becomes of Earl Summerfield? Soon it'll be my birthday. What sort of person will I be at 27? Think of myself at the age of 40! Think of myself at 60.

Eleven o'clock. I can't collect my thoughts tonight, usually I do. Usually I feel Rounded. It could be the food, tasted unpleasant—yesterday's food on the forks and spoons. I wonder if Bianca washed them or just gave them a quick rinse. I've noticed it before but not so strong. I think my senses are becoming more acute. Often have the feeling that I perceive more now than in the past. Veins seem apparent beneath my skin & occasionally I distinguish the bones. Do I delude myself? No, I don't think so.

Back and forth. Am I worried about Bianca? The conference ought to be over by this time. She said they had the fall semester to discuss, and of course she'll be reminding Spach that she's capable of an administrative job. If she does get promoted I think I'll leave the Bureau and look for a more important job. Maybe I should have done that several years ago, I'm being turned into stone. Saturdays and Sundays plus evenings. That should be enough free time. Yes, I could amount to something. Heard about a taxicab driver who studied singing and became a Broadway musical star. It wasn't luck, it was ambition. Magnus thinks the next vase he examines on McAllister Street or the next chipped table or the next tarnished snuffbox or whatever—a button, a lump of lead—the very next one's going to be a rare treasure that will make him rich. He's wrong, which is why he'll never

159

amount to a thing. Never get out. Gray, feeble & lost. I won't make the same mistake. I'm not afraid to Work my way up in the world. Just suppose Bianca becomes school vice-principal, then a few years later she'll force her way onto the Board of Education, but by then I could be equally important. The thing is, I've got to decide. Decide what I'm meant to be! Not what I am, what I should have been. Yes, tomorrow I'll—footsteps & her key in the lock.

JULY 23

Opened the door last night prepared for the worst. I know she's been wondering about me, I know from her expression because I've turned around suddenly and caught her staring. The next time she questions me I'll fling certain questions right back in her face. Instead of keeping my fist in my pocket I'll let her have a look at the truth. That's forbidden, this is forbidden, etc. But what does she offer in place of it? I'm not as simple as she thinks. If I had a gun last night I'd have shot as soon as she stepped inside. After which I think I might have cut out her tongue and nailed it against the wall. However, I should realize by this time that whenever you're afraid something's going to happen it never does. Smiled and brushed my cheek with her lips just as if she was glad to be home, in fact glad to see me. And today she's got a new hair style—the first change in how many years? Calls it a French roll, or twist or some such. She told me after I asked but can't recall exactly what she said. I noticed that she seemed surprised I was interested in her hair. Does she think I never notice what she looks like? Eyes widened and she placed her hands on her hips as she used to do just after we got married—I'd forgotten how she did that, it's been so long. I was positive she wanted to kiss me. Several moments we stood there looking at each

160

other. She mentioned the name of the hair style, I nodded. I should have spoken. I did want to say something nice but my jaws were locked up tight as a bank vault. After a while she shrugged, face got hard as a statue and she walked into the kitchen, so nothing came of it.

What I could do is make an outline, or some sort of list, perhaps explaining problems to be discussed. Leave this information where she'd be certain to find it—on her plate, for example. That ought to clarify our relationship.

JULY 24

Lately everything's been remote. I set down thoughts that occur or that I've Willed to appear but they don't leave much more trace than steam in a spout. I could set down my name & age, address of the Bureau, habits of Bianca, six hundred additional facts. To what end? For what purpose? It's a waste of time. I've squandered a thousand hours sitting at this desk with my head in my hands or drawing pictures on the windowpane. Every night I sit here gazing into the darkness while Bianca reads in the bedroom and smokes & smokes. Will both of us finally be buried in ashes?

Perhaps I should sit here motionless for the rest of my existence, motionless as the dwarf marigold. It's dying. I suppose it's root-bound. I say to myself that I ought to have a look. I could remove it & plant it in a larger pot, add new soil, but for some reason I'm not able to. The leaves are wilting, already a few have fallen.

JULY 25

Bianca says I should go on a diet. Past few weeks I've put on weight, no doubt about that but it isn't serious. I

161

believe she just wants to meddle with me, she's got to involve herself in my life. True they're all alike, committed to some sort of intercourse with us, otherwise they wither & fade.

JULY 26

Talk of women, rattle of nuts in a bottle. Possessions. Clothes. Liquids. I've watched them scattering grain for pigeons in Union Square. I've read letters they've written, looked at their babies. Yes, and I've listened to them sing. That's the only time I love them.

JULY 27

Saturday, up late, almost noon, B had gone out. Felt tense and congested even before opening my eyes. I was dreaming & recall telling myself I shouldn't forget the dream. Details were escaping every instant but I planned to memorize whatever remained. Most of the afternoon was occupied with repeating aloud as much as could be remembered. I thought that by doing this I'd save the fragments but it didn't work—they got away, which is puzzling. If I said to myself just as I was waking up: "Go to the laundry at 5 o'clock!" there'd be no trouble remembering. Why should dreams escape?

Well, that one did. This morning I could have recited a dozen details, after lunch almost as many. But now at a quarter to midnight I'd have to concentrate to call up anything worth mentioning. Dark forces are at work. However, one gets accustomed to them. Currents in the ocean. Vast calms. Mouths of rivers that we never know exist. Maybe I should write a letter to one of those scientific magazines suggesting some sort of permanent dye ought to be developed, then parts of the ocean could be dyed and all the mysterious currents could be charted. It would be very useful. In fact this could open up a new career for me, writing scientific articles, etc.

So another day ends & in general it was unsatisfactory. Stiff with discontent, gorged with fluid. Went to Spreckels Lake for a while, played with basketballs at the amusement park, rode the carrousel, caterpillar, electric scooters. Stopped to chat with a mounted policeman and was patting his horse when suddenly I felt surrounded by female organs. Into the toilet for a minute, then walked home very weak & thoughtful. No matter where I go or what I try to do I can't get away. Remember reading somewhere of four things that can never be satisfied. The first three I've forgotten, the fourth was the mouth of the womb, but I think there must be five—and the fifth is the mouth of the mind.

JULY 28

I wish Bianca knew about me. I wish I could tell her. I wish. I want.

JULY 29

Yesterday my birthday—27. She didn't mention it and she didn't give me a present. I guess that must be her way of reminding me that I'd forgotten hers. The difference is that I forgot, but she didn't. I hope she's satisfied, hope she feels revenged. Should I tell her that nothing she can do or say to me has the slightest effect? Or should I let her believe the insult was successful?

163

JULY 30

Had it out with her. She says she loves me, but the things I do have made her sick. Always she manages to make me feel ashamed. Everything's my fault. No matter what happens I'm to blame. I don't believe she loves me. I believe not a word she says.

JULY 31

It was very hot today. After work I got some ice cream, after which rode a streetcar straight from downtown to the beach where I walked around in the sand and thought about several things. There was fog lying offshore as though if you sailed out that far you'd go off the edge of the world. I didn't come to any decisions, just felt tired and discouraged, finally rode the streetcar back to 16th Avenue & walked the rest of the way. July is over.

AUGUST 1

I think I'll go to the planetarium this next Saturday or Sunday to distract myself, my head's about to roll away & I guess it's been affecting my work as well as my appearance. Fensdeicke stopped by this afternoon, coughed delicately and patted her lips and smiled, then said just loud enough of course for everybody else to hear that the Bureau "does like us to keep up appearances"—after which she let me wait. She just let me wait. Knew I was forced to Ask. That way I was on the defensive from the beginning. She enjoys keeping people in the dark. Why didn't she come right out and tell me what was wrong? But oh no—had to have her grain of satisfaction. And the only thing she could find to criticize was that my shoes needed polishing. Had to catch my breath because I wasn't sure if I was going to break down crying or if I was going to kill her. The whole thing was so unnecessary. Why did she need to do it? Why? Why?

AUGUST 2

Over & under! Upside down! I feel like a dwarf dancing for his life.

165

AUGUST 3

More blood, more cruelty. Body of an old Howard Street bum found in some weeds behind a billboard. Mouth stuffed full of dirt and grass, little burns all over his face, palms, soles of his feet—cigarette burns. Several people in the neighborhood said they heard scuffling but didn't pay much attention to it, also noticed some boys running away. And that's how it ended. Well, look out for everybody. Look out for all of us.

Don't know what sort of reality this is. But it is. Reality of ordinary people. Oh, perhaps the day is going to come when we'll be as orderly as a herd of cattle with electrodes planted in the brain. Then of course all of the famous philosophical arguments won't mean very much—not when anybody can be altered by a few sparks of electricity. However that's a long way off, at least as we measure time. For the present we're going to go on this way, robbing, torturing. Trust nobody, least of all the holy Self.

What thou understandest not, thou shalt know in the day of visitation. That's right.

So I lock the door to another day but can't exactly say much was accomplished. That's usually how it is. Some interesting thoughts but of course thoughts aren't always beneficial. Call this a higgledy-piggledy day and go to bed.

AUGUST 4

Doing my work with the usual dispatch yet cannot escape the feeling that I'm being observed. Not only the supervisors, but also Vladimir's been watching me, and I think he's talking about me to McAuliffe. Just why this is, I can't say. Little doubt that Fensdeicke trots around me with a lighter foot ever since last week when I whispered that she'd better leave me alone. She looked as though I'd slapped her, scurried back to her desk without a word. Six months ago I'd have licked the floor sooner than say what I did.

Or maybe I imagine too much, and my sensibilities have been affected. I'm tired & nervous. So many thoughts press upon me, in spite of the fact I don't have anything particular to worry about. What reason could I have to fear the future? None. I look forward to the coming months, yes, and to many years of life.

AUGUST 5

Monday. Am convinced that the history of Mankind is the story of One opposed by many. When a slave asserts himself it must be for the sake of others. Yes. That's how it is.

AUGUST 6

I've been right all along. Signaling in the office. Fensdeicke & Aneurine are indeed signaling to each other. Few minutes before 2 this P.M. happened to glance toward A and noticed that she was tapping her teeth with a pencil, glanced next to F and discovered she was watching me. I'm not as simple as they think. Clegg's in on it, the way he turns his head their direction when he coughs. He always coughs twice, never more than that. Very seldom. Very seldom indeed. What does it mean? The only thing I can be sure of is that I'm the intended sacrifice. Assuming that's so, how much time remains? Should I make plans, or not? The forces of evil are too powerful to be overcome by the plans of an individual, just as the energies of our system are going to decay & the glory of the sun be dimmed. Then the earth, which will be tideless and inert, will not tolerate the race which for a few moments disturbed its solitude. Man goes down into the Pit, all his thoughts perish, and his uneasy conscience which has for a brief space broken the silence of the universe will be eternally at rest. Matter will know itself no further. And these things that we call Imperishable Monuments and Immortal Deeds—yes, and death itself, and love that we thought more powerful than death, will be as if they had not ever been. Nor will anything that is be better or worse.

AUGUST 7

To the beach this pleasant evening and left footprints in the sand. They'll be visible a few days, I've marked the boundary of the tide. Pelicans sculled across, gulls made high wrinkles above the cliff. There was a breeze from the south and I stood for a while watching ships glide through the Golden Gate as though bound for the Holy Land. I remember reading somewhere a long time ago that the Crusaders didn't travel to Jerusalem to visit Christ's sepulcher as they thought they did, but to deliver themselves of terrible forces within—they'd lived so long under the weight of northern mist they somehow knew the pilgrimage was necessary, the alternative was Madness. Peacocks, date palms, carpets & mosques & foreign women who touched their eyes with kohl. Sacks of ivory. Gold. Sacred relics. Jewels heavier than iron coins, goblets crusted with diamonds! Yes, that's how their passions were controlled, order delivered out of chaos. Breath of our first existence.

Perhaps it's true that Man must close his eyes in order to

168

see. Changing light & color, we must be prisms. Who can describe us who hasn't seen us from every side? Hmm. Well, as somebody once remarked, there are plays that can't be performed. Yes, and a good many lines already memorized won't be spoken. At least that's the way I look at it.

AUGUST 8

Woke up a few minutes before dawn this morning. Can't say exactly whether it was the dream that woke me, or the silence, or possibly even the silence of the dream. I don't quite know. But I suddenly opened my eyes & knew I had been standing in front of an old cabinet of some sort— maybe it was a walnut desk. I think that's what it was—yes, I've begun to remember it. A cherrywood desk with some red or blue flowers painted on it, and there were scratches in the varnish. Maybe the cat scratched it. Trying to remember what the desk smelled like, but cannot. I was pulling out the drawers one after another, reaching in and feeling around for something. What did I want? Next I began thinking about an old house with thick carpets on the floor. Aunt Ollie took me there late Sunday afternoon to visit an old lady who asked me my name. It was on a Sunday I know because of the suit I was wearing. I must have told her my name because she picked up a box from the table beside her chair and said, "Earl, this jewel casket is for you." It was a green leather box shaped like a fan with a border of gold fleurs-de-lis. I took it & walked away, then sat down in a dark corner of the house holding the box in both hands and wondered what kind of jewels were inside and how big they were. I thought the old lady had given me jewels worth millions of dollars. I thought I would make something for her, I would make an airplane or a kite. I decided that the box must be full of diamonds because diamonds were more precious than rubies or emeralds or sapphires. I thought I would find some little diamonds strung together and large ones with different shapes, and probably also the biggest diamond in the world. I had a book with pictures of famous diamonds so I knew their names—one called the Nassak and for some reason I thought it might be in the box I was holding. I thought she could have gotten it from a Hindu temple, or maybe from a British officer with a black mustache who swaggered around in the jungle with a stick under his arm. Then I thought about the Excelsior and the Jubilee and the Victoria and the Star of Africa. Thought one of those might be in the box. I remember I wasn't in a hurry to open it because as soon as it was opened I wouldn't be able to think about what might be inside, so held it in my hands a long time. Mmm—don't believe I opened it until Aunt Ollie called that we were leaving, then put my thumbs side by side & pulled them apart & the box jumped open—remember now the way it jumped. Inside weren't any jewels, just a dark red velvet mound with a groove running through it. Tried to put my face into the box, remember rubbing my nose against the velvet. I guess nothing else ever gave me as much pleasure.

Don't know why this all came back to me. Dream of an hour long past. Somehow it makes me sad, makes me wonder who I am. Earl Summerfield's just a name.

AUGUST 9

Prayer & solitude & meditation. Maybe it's not too late to change myself, not if that's what I actually want. My blood's been blacker than burnt sulphur and I was sick with disgusting smells but am going to be somebody else from now on.

170

AUGUST 10

Outside the center of Self. Not what I want to be. Repeating that those who are saved cannot commit a crime. Yet always the hand of him that betrayeth me is with me on this table.

AUGUST 11

Black as a night of the Middle Ages. Fog swirling overhead, cold wind from the ocean. The moon burns dim and green. I hear mice scuttling in the kitchen. It seems to me I've lived before, but how or when I couldn't say. My heart feels greasy, heavy as a lump of coal. Endless discontent.

As for tomorrow, don't think about it. I'll wear dark glasses & stuff cotton in my ears.

AUGUST 12

Good morning, Mr. Summerfield! Good morning, Miss Aneurine! Good morning, Mr. Clegg. Morning, McAuliffe. But we're all the same. Underneath that crust of cordiality we're bubbling with ideas of revenge. Oh yes. Each one of us. Take our esteemed District Attorney—claims the assault on Loretta Lengfeldt was the most shocking crime etc. etc. etc. in the many years of his experience etc. etc. and furthermore etc. he isn't going to have any compunction about demanding the death sentence for Peter Brandt, vicious depraved killer etc. No more hesitation about asking the supreme penalty than if Brandt was a ser-

THE DIARY OF A RAPIST

pent—a serpent—a serpent! Old film tangled in the reel. Meanwhile the vicious killer works crossword puzzles in his cell, also spends quite a lot of time examining his new mustache in the mirror, apparently unconcerned, a fact which annoys authorities and citizens both. My guess is that he's fascinated by himself but doesn't want to let them know. Then too he's mildly amused as well as impressed that he's on the front page of every newspaper. Why should he be concerned? There's no doubt in his mind about what will happen. They've got him & he knows it. Her schoolbooks in his car, the bracelet in his house. And caught telling terrible lies. They're exasperated that he lies so casually, smiles whenever they trip him up. Bland and creamy, soft as a fresh orange blossom, every bit as tender as the little victim. Poses agreeably for the camera. Nothing matters now, remembering his pleasure. Weeks, months, years & years in prison—he'd enjoy that but looks forward even more to a few instants of excitement in the painted steel chamber. Uniformed guards, signals, mysterious rituals. Blessing of the priest as Christ and the Devil join. Powerful sodomy. Hail once again to the hieroglyphic State machine. Oh yes, he knows it all. I read his face as easily as I read my own, despite the differences. Caressing the microphone when it was held near his lips—certainly no need to be told much more. He's far too sensual for the world. If they let him loose he'd do it again. Tits like the first horns on a calf, drops of virgin blood seeping through the slit—violence, violence! However, he won't get loose. The State knows and Peter Brandt knows, which is why he sits around with hands complacently folded in his lap like an Asiatic holy man waiting for what's to be.

Well, all of us do face the Lord High Executioner sooner or later, I suppose what puzzles me is the arrogance of the State.

Ho hum. Might as well go to bed.

AUGUST

AUGUST 13

Life begins to seem like a stone under water.

AUGUST 14

Whatever is done in the service of love is justifiable, whether this is felt toward one person or whether it happens in response to a feeling toward all of humanity.

AUGUST 15

When I think about what I used to be—when I consider my past ideas it seems like they've fused into a puddle of warm metal. They don't have the slightest value.

I guess it must be this faculty for recognizing our mistakes that finally will permit us to lift ourselves from the present sink. If not & we fail, at least there's still a multitude of planets among which God may choose.

AUGUST 16

Impelled to set down my daily note, though the sun's nicely above the Pacific. Usually I wait till dark when thoughts have clarified and sunk like sand to the bottom. Now I'm too anxious. Have just recently noticed this bowl of eggs and am wondering how long it's been here. Or Bianca's scissors. Well!—both worth considering. Indeed there's very little that escapes my notice.

173

THE DIARY OF A RAPIST

AUGUST 17

What's bubbled through my brain these past few nights? Every word senseless!

The fact of the matter is that several times I've come upon myself standing like a savage with my hands pressed against my ears. I suppose it's the noise. The noise never stops. Or could it be the lies and hatred everywhere?

Feel like a little spider suspended beneath a strand. Nobody sees me. Nobody's aware. I mean nothing to anybody on earth. Earl Summerfield? Who's that? Suicide or Counterfeit?

AUGUST 18

Couldn't sleep last night. Spent hours observing self in the bathroom mirror wondering how I've changed. Would anyone looking at me now know that I'm not what I used to be?

Isn't it odd that we march down our days until abruptly we're shocked! Yes, and further shocked. A thing occurs in our presence yet we remain unaware until it's much too obvious. Say X is trundled off to the hospital suffering from incurable this-or-that. A force was nibbling toward the soul, yet who perceived it? Or some seed planted in us at birth has come slowly to fruition while we stood around gossiping. I confess I marvel—indeed I often wonder at our substance —what it is. Fragments of a precious bowl shattered on the floor?

Well, in any case, back to the office tomorrow.

174

AUGUST 19

Argument at lunch. Aneurine passionately insisting Brandt was falsely accused. A plot, she insists. That's nonsense of course and I told her so. Some mysterious person put the girl's books into his car, she says. "And the bracelet in his house?" I asked quite sarcastically. I thought that would shut her up but I spoke out of place. She's angry. It was foolish of me to talk so much. I can't afford to be making enemies, certainly not of somebody in her position. It's possible that I ruined my career by a single remark. There's no way of telling, but I'd better apologize, explain that I really should have been listening instead of sounding officious. Yes, that's a good idea. I'll tell her I'm sorry, then see what effect That produces.

Peter Brandt. How different we are, he and I. He's selfish and he's amoral, I'm not. In fact I'm quite the opposite. He doesn't care about us. He cares for nothing except those murky female passages, I care more about an almond shell. Yet if that's so why am I not disturbed by what he did? I can't decide—it's too difficult. All I'm sure of is that he acted out a familiar wish & that's enough for the State to kill him. Such ceremonial masks we wear.

Midnight news. Student nurse waiting for a taxi outside of Mt. Zion when two boys approached, took her by the arms and dragged her around the corner into a vacant house where the customary performance took place. Tomorrow the usual outcries but in two weeks it'll be forgotten. We think the significant event's the latest.

AUGUST 20

Another and another and another and now another one today, this time across the bay in Oakland. Some housewife snatched from a street corner while carrying a bag of groceries. Man jumped out of a car and slapped her twice across the face, pushed her into the car and drove away while people stood watching, reassuring themselves that it must have been her husband. Hours later the corpse was discovered in a Negro Baptist church. She'd been strangled with a length of electric cord. Hands tied by her own black silk stockings. Naked, slashed from breast to belly, her blood had formed a pool in the aisle and she was dangling above it, suspended from the balcony. She'd been elevated because we must elevate what we worship. Yes, it's a further diagram of rage, not much else. Dusty light filters through leaded windows. Stifled groans & pleas. Everything's ordained by our desire for life.

AUGUST 21

Reflecting on the incident of yesterday, I believe it might have been those stockings that caused her death. That could have been enough. I've noticed how women suggest themselves. They never tire of hinting to us about the dark flower within. And I've seen how they choose to stand as they wait for the changing light, yes. And the clumsy movement of their legs—that explains to us how overcome they are by the need for motion. There's this quality about them that stirs some force inside us. We wish to cause them suffering & death. Furthermore I believe they sense this, yet they continue to accept us. It's what I've never compre-

176

hended—their phlegmatic willingness. Mmm—agreement. Whatever it is. That afternoon, don't know how many years ago, sixteen or seventeen probably, tied Patsy to the fence and sprayed her with the garden hose. She screamed when the water hit her, then quit struggling, sagged against the rope and looked at me with a peculiar expression. I still see her eyes. She knew something I didn't. Had the feeling she was keeping a secret from me. Went up and poked her stomach with the nozzle and squirted everywhere. She wouldn't talk to me. Forgot how it ended. Somebody else untied her because I didn't. Anyway it was her fault. She suggested it. Unclean. Unclean. Unclean. Unclean.

AUGUST 22

Thursday. Very hot afternoon. Reminded me of prophecies. Clouds of smoke over the city—Gomorrah burning because we have gotten fat and sleek, slippery with Evil. Picture in the paper of airplanes dropping bombs like eggs oozing from the tail of beetles. Whatever happens to us we deserve & have brought upon ourselves. Fiery gas, poison, bomb, arrogance & false piety. Mock justice. Yes, it's on the way. Fires will break out, animals give up their lairs, women bear monsters, salt in sweet water! Victims of own ignorance—yes, that's how it is & not long to wait. Final retribution.

This heat, throbbing in my skull. I can see myself dangling and swaying at the end of a thread or piece of colored string. Now a message has been written on the door. My knees feel bloody. This room smells. I'm sick, no use to pray.

AUGUST 23

Nervous and sucked dry. Looking forward to the end of this week, of this month. Ancient gods reign within our hearts now as they always have.

AUGUST 24

State Assembly considering a bill that would permit wives of criminals to visit overnight—common practice elsewhere in the world, but for America a disturbing thought. Fucking in jail. I suppose we'd rather not inspect the blossoms of the psyche. However, the lotus must flower whether we recognize it or we don't & only Christians believe that a man deprived of a woman doesn't eventually settle on another man. Just the same, the bill won't pass. Blackmail and sodomy continue.

What other news this Saturday? Have a look. District Attorney's positive Brandt will be convicted. Brandt himself goes on smiling gently toward the camera—silken dreamer. Probably tubercular. In any event, what's done was delicate & private, now he plays this involuted game for his own amusement. He scattered clues enough for 6, perhaps bemused it took the officers so long to locate him. Day by day my respect for Authority decreases, and yet beyond a certain point it's more some kind of sympathy that I feel. So much for that—what the Law can do to him has naught to do with me. In the first place, I'm not exactly captured. Who's going to catch me if I don't choose to catch myself? Nobody.

I could tell the papers that I wear glasses when I read,

although at times I don't. I'm growing bald & my ears are unusually large. My lips are red, I pout a bit. Give them that, let them worry. See if they uncover me. Eh! Eh!

AUGUST 25

Recently have not had much appetite. Bowels weak & heart flutters. At times I think I must be trickling through a maze like a steel ball or a pellet of mercury. Voices merge with echoing buildings. Certain afternoons I'm sure I've smelled those trees in the park a mile away. As though my body was attempting to warn me. I know that I've judged harshly, that I rage & fret like some early Jesuit disgusted by the nature of humanity, but still I can recognize my name and think I'll be all right. Probably the cause of it is this hot weather.

AUGUST 26

Tonight walked around for several hours—tennis courts, college for women, etc.—reflecting that the month has practically escaped & I've used it stupidly. Should have been applying myself, my life can't keep on like this. Well, I've worked too hard, yes, and been exhausted when I got home—that's why there's not much left of August. Days squandered. Days asking the same questions of the same imbeciles, embarrassing to recognize a face and know I asked the same question a week ago. How long have you been out of work? Applied for work on your own initiative? Previously applied for unemployment compensation? How long a resident of the State of California? And those smart alecs that ask the questions themselves! As if if was My fault. As if I was the one who insisted on going over it every week. I'd process them in a hurry if the Bureau didn't insist on Procedure. Can't even explain to them that I'm forced to ask every question. No wonder they think I'm a fool. Maybe it's what I really am. What kind of a life is this? What am I doing in the Bureau? Why am I there? I'm much too important to be going to that office every day.

Try to forget. Other places aren't any better. Dirty businesses. Dirtier people. Doesn't do much good to shake your fist out the window. If so, at what? Murder, war, theft, usury, greed, slander & impiety—to say the least. More than any month requires. September's going to be identical. And what should I do? Sit on my stool another year? I'm 27, twice that is 54. By then what will I have learned that I don't already know. The time's come to take a look at yourself, Earl Summerfield. Take a look at yourself! Do that! Yes, oh yes!

AUGUST 27

Not many things on earth affect us as much as the sight of a certain person. Yesterday I was discouraged & could think of few reasons to go on living but now instead of looking back I can only think about the future. Why? Just because accidentally I saw a woman on the street. A certain woman. I'm positive that's who it was. The light changed before I could get close enough to make sure but something inside of me is convinced. One glimpse through the crowd. A glimpse of M. St. J. talking to a man—must have been her fianceé because he looked the part. Yes, muscular & crewcut, of course that's who it was.

Well, I've tried to hide my feeling, keep it out of sight, but I may as well admit the fact—I'm jealous. I'd kill him if I could. The first time I've ever seen Harold Schenke but wouldn't hesitate to murder him. I sit here hating him, so sick & weak with jealousy I can't even clench my fist. No matter which direction I turn my head I see that face. He's so sure of himself, that's what I hate. He's got everything he wants. Try to push him away from me but I'm pushing at a shadow. Thinking of her by herself was bad enough but now the two of them! Yes, I'm jealous. Some feelings we mistake, but nobody's ever called That by another name.

If only I knew how she felt about me! Well, I know where she lives. I could go there. I could see her again. Tell her I'm coming?

AUGUST 28

Wednesday. Caught doodling. Mrs. Fensdeicke simply crept up in back of me. Probably guessed I wasn't listening. No wonder, it's a story I've heard too many many times—construction finished, crew laid off, 65th on the union list, etc. etc. I could recite it to the last detail. And there I sat jotting down that bitch's name again and again.

I wonder what else I've done. What else have people noticed? I've been so sure that I could control myself, now I'm wondering. I need to talk to somebody, but I have nobody to talk to. Not one person on earth.

AUGUST 29

Back and forth with bits of paper in my ears, trying not to think. Did I see her the other day, or not? I argue that it wasn't—somebody resembled her—then argue back

181

again, tormenting myself. Back & forth learning what distances we travel in a narrow room.

I know that I need to visit her as much as I despise her. I can't believe she hates me. Why did she catch my wrist when I got ready to leave?—and she did, yes, I didn't make that up. She wanted me to stay. Or was it just some instinct saying she didn't want to be alone? I need to know, but how shall I find out? Would she recognize me if I went back? I think so—yes, my face she might or might not know, in either case she'd guess. She'd know me in an instant, there's an inner certainty about such things. A century from this date she'd recognize me.

Thinking about what V once said—Aphrodite arose from the dismembered arm of her father when it was cast into the sea, which means that love is born through violence. Is that true or not? If not, how can it be that our lives are changed? —I'm different than I was six weeks ago, so is she. How is she different than she was? Until I meet her again I can't be sure. As for myself, I feel the blackness oozing out. I'd like to tell her, explain to her what I've been as well as what I hope to be. Nothing else is so important.

Midnight. Church bells & the city obscured by fog.

AUGUST 30

The feeling continues to grow like a leafy plant, like a fern in the depths of my soul. She does belong to me. We two were formed on purpose, we alone reflect the Universe.

Day breaks & shadows flee away.

182

AUGUST

AUGUST 31

Oh Jesus when I think about her!—think of another kind of life. Think of her nakedness & all! Think of the letters of her name—even that's enough.

I'll send her a gift. What's appropriate? Jewels are cold, with undertones of death. I could send her a pebble washed by the ocean. Or the wing of a white seagull.

SEPTEMBER 1

God knows how many miles I walked with 2 nickels in my hand. Stopped at one telephone booth, then another, each time finding reasons not to call. What if she didn't recognize my voice—or what if she did? Other, deeper reasons, and I found them because usually we find whatever we need, it's not difficult. Wondering also about the purse & whether she thinks of me as a thief. That's what she thought at first—clutching it against her belly. Trying to hide it! A few months ago that woman hit by the taxi, lying in the street half drowned in her own blood but still gripping the purse. Somehow it means more to them than it does to us. Maybe that's how I'd feel about a gun. Anyway, I didn't think about it until I noticed her trying to hide it, then I didn't have much choice—remember shouting, grabbing for it. That's when it opened and spilled—she let go as soon as things began spilling out. I guess that's when she fell down, started crying, said I'd hurt her knee. No, am not sure. Later? She fell down before I hit her. Or afterward? Was waiting to see if she was going to faint. Yes, I hoped so, excited by the popping noise of slapped flesh. Eyes open. She thought I was planning to kill her, no doubt of it, but I think also she was curious—the way she stared. That was when I should have talked to her. In fact I could have pretended I was suffering—then she'd have gotten sympathetic. They can't stay angry with a man who's suffering, it goes against their nature. Yes, that was the time to reach her. Seems like I always miss my chance. I wonder what I looked like. Why did she stare at me? Wish I'd had a mirror to see my face. Usually I know just exactly how I look, compose my features to present myself as I choose to be, but certain times I suppose our expression gets away. Probably I looked impressive. That's why she kept quiet instead of screaming. She respected me—hadn't thought of that until now but there's no other possible explanation. Wish I'd seen myself. Grinding my teeth like a horse, face twisted out of shape, etc. Anybody would be afraid. Yes. But on the other hand that isn't the truth, my eyes were as big as hers, also must admit doing what I didn't mean to do. Smell of my insides & the shame—hopping around so she wouldn't notice, jabbering all the time. Jabber jabber jabber but what did I say? Told her all beauty queens are whores & that's the truth because there's plenty of evidence. Six months ago in the park inviting me! Well, I told her she got what she deserved, got what she asked for. Brought the whole thing on herself. I never knew she existed until she got up there and paraded around displaying her charms in Public. If that isn't the sign of a whore, what is! She couldn't answer me. She didn't even try! I'm not surprised of course. No, I'm not surprised. I did the right thing. Furthermore, she realized what was going to happen—oh yes!—last February staring at me. Inviting me. Immorality revealed by her eyelids. I knew right away the sort she was. Well, what I should have done was take all of her clothes and throw them into the ocean. I felt sorry for her but I won't again. In fact what I should have done was start with the shears at her bottom and open her up like a fish.

Out again. Called but didn't wait for an answer, just the same probably she guessed who it was.

185

SEPTEMBER 2

I've decided she made use of me. I was what she wanted. Earl Summerfield. Everybody admits the depth of a woman's hypocrisy has never been found. Pretending to struggle, begging for time to pray—not for herself, oh no, for ME. Thinking she could trick me, but I know her with her foxy nose and white chubby cheeks and that beehive of honey hair—not much about her I couldn't describe, not much. And the ugliness of her mind, yes, that's what makes me wonder just how many others she's had. How many others like me? How many before poor Earl? How many since? Also, what else is there I don't know about? Probably she lied about her age and worked in those clubs along Mason Street, sold herself for 3 dollars. More than anything it's this hypocrisy of women that brings a taste of slime to my mouth.

SEPTEMBER 3

Tonight's Chronicle has a picture of some actress dancing practically naked on a nightclub table. In my opinion that represents Woman as she is.

The more I think about it the less I doubt.

SEPTEMBER 4

Mentioned picture of the actress to McA. He'd seen it, naturally, and says all of them love to exhibit their bodies, love to perform, never satisfied. Since then have been thinking about that moment when she arched her back, shoving with her heels—bent herself into a half circle. Reminded me of hysterical nuns in the Middle Ages. Yes, McA's right, nothing stops the obscene performance.

SEPTEMBER 5

Floated around the place—yes, exactly how it was! but didn't see her. Did she guess I might be there? If so, did she also guess what I was going to do? Sometimes I have the feeling she knows more about me than I suspect. How? All the same, it's possible. But of course there could be other reasons she wasn't there tonight. She might be sick, or ashamed of the disgusting way she's lived, lies she's told, etc. Also, she could be setting a trap. Foolish to visit the church so often, I'm no smarter than an ape playing with a dirty rag. Caution, caution. I'll stop thinking about her. No sooner said than done.

The clock in the hall just struck ten. Bianca's not yet back from the school. Told me yesterday she'd be late, something about another conference with Spach. Then he takes her out for coffee so she might not get in until midnight.

Apartment silent as a tomb.

A mouse went scuttling across the floor a few moments ago & I'm still out of breath. Hopped to my feet and rushed around the room waving my arms, shouting, threatening her life but she wasn't terribly frightened, only pretended to be. She knew it was a joke. Also, she knows who's clumsy & slow afoot. Squeezed under the door, scurried down the hall and hid somewhere in the kitchen. I went looking for her on hands and knees and heard the palpitations of her heart but the kitchen was too dark to find her. Returned to the desk after bolting the door. B's annoyed by the bolt but I can't

187

stand the idea of a person being able to walk in on me. She'd like nothing better—nothing she wants more than access to my life.

SEPTEMBER 6

I wonder if a man's mind finally can drive him mad. My thoughts go bounding across each other like tigers in a circus. What causes me to imagine so much? I ought to take an interest in—yes, Earl, in what! In what? The Bureau used to seem important. Possibilities of advancement, ingratiating yourself with the supervisors and with Mr. Foxx, but I don't care about it any longer. Put in my day, ride home to this silent place. Ride home with the flapping of black wings.

Does Bianca try to help me? One glance at her face reminds me never to beg. We don't belong together. Why did I think so? Because she told me, there wasn't any other reason. She sounded so—well, so positive. How wrong our life together has been. Bitterness untold. I couldn't begin. Poisonous leaves, suppurating fruit, and now my brain's fixed on a woman who must hate me. Useless to persuade myself otherwise. I've injured her, she won't forget. Besides, I mean nothing. It doesn't matter if I risked my life. I cry out loud that she loves me, but at the same time I don't believe it.

God give me to say what I suffer. The more I'm stripped the more I feel the pain.

SEPTEMBER 7

Tevis Lincoln carried headfirst to the execution chamber too terrified to walk, couldn't speak, according to the Chronicle. Groaned and mumbled, tried to repeat his childhood prayers. Seems to me that was the 4th or maybe the 5th time they tried to get rid of him, something or other always prevented it, but of course the State doesn't give up. Once it sets its mind to a thing not much short of another Deluge can stop the machinery. Well, I can't remember Mr. Lincoln's crime, it's very vague now, happened several years ago. Shot his wife to death in a bowling alley, I believe. Something of the sort. I do remember the first time he was scheduled he wrestled with the guards who were trying to strap him into the chair. One of the witnesses had a heart attack. Must have been quite a spectacle. Can't recall what saved him then, anyway this morning at 8 after 10 they managed to gas him. Newspaper says he wanted to take his banjo into the chamber but the request was denied. I guess it would make the spectators uncomfortable—a banjo leaning against the chair while Lincoln choked to death. Somehow the whole affair reminds me of those medieval animal trials —pig dressed in smock & trousers, snout chopped off and a mask over its head so that it would resemble a man. Enough evidence presented to convict it, next the sentencing and next the torture, finally the execution in a suitable public square. Alas, poor pig, all he ever wanted was an average life. It's puzzling.

SEPTEMBER 8

Voices on every side. Sometimes I think I'll drown in a sea of voices. On the street, in the office, none of it makes sense. The voices of spiders in a jar, biting each other to death. McA goes on & on about secret aphrodisiacs, filthy shows, weekends he's spent grunting against some fat bottom. I stare at him with contempt but he decides I want to hear more. V talks about the government, socialism, etc.

I don't care about that either. Sick to death of Magnus and old Clegg and the rest of them. Look around suddenly and ask myself where I am. I seem to be flying above them, weightless as a paper kite.

SEPTEMBER 9

Corpse of Chinese woman discovered in a vacant building, stabbed stabbed stabbed a hundred times. Madness of flesh against itself. Why do we prey on what we need? And yesterday, or was it the day before?—man sentenced to death for murdering his 90-year-old father. Judge denied motion for a new trial & announced the penalty after listening to three psychiatrists testify. One said he was insane, another said he wasn't, and the last one said he was— but only for a little while. So it continues, typical of our time. Discrepancies & wild assumption. Danger to the ocean lies in whirling water. Keep watch. Keep watch, Earl Summerfield.

SEPTEMBER 10

If God has truly ordered the universe Man cannot do wrong. It is He who points out the direction to us & establishes the power of choice. It is He who places within our sight the objects of desire. Wherever we turn our faces we see what He has created. I believe this.

SEPTEMBER 11

Last night after reading I rode downtown and sat for a long while in Union Square wondering what I ought to do. Wednesday night and many people walked by but not one of them paid any attention to me, nor did I pay any attention to them. What could they teach me? It isn't that I despise them for walking back and forth, I didn't feel anything toward them—nothing at all, unless indifference is a sort of feeling. One asked me for a cigarette. Shrugged & looked away, had absolutely no wish to speak. I don't have a word to say to anybody. If I did speak to them they'd ignore me. If I said to them that the days are fast approaching when a kingdom shall rise on earth and it will be more terrible than all the kingdoms before it, would they listen? If I got up on the bench and shouted at them, would they listen? Of course not, so I sat among them silently. Speech isn't necessary. Scientists have pointed out that people were on earth struggling and eating and fighting and so forth for at least half a million years without making a sound. Speech means you're determined to lie, so believe nothing anybody says. Trust yourself above all others. When people make offerings turn away your face from them.

SEPTEMBER 12

Maybe it's the presence of V on the next stool, is that it? If not, what? The Bureau seems so absolutely Unreal. Everybody obsessed by thoughts of promotion, rank, until I can't—or is it quite the opposite? Ech ech ech! We may be figures in a yellowing myth—our pens scratching along under fluorescent lights, now and then the rattle of a bottle sliding down the trough of the Coke machine. Every time I hear that noise it frightens me. It's like a warning & I've had warnings enough—two attacks of dizziness, other little things, instants quickly gone but alarming just the same. Surprise myself behaving queerly, as though I'm not actually who I know I am. Earl Summerfield. Earl Summer-

191

field. Yes. I'm still a miserable clerk and don't have any more dreams about becoming what I wasn't destined to be. Don't suppose I'll ever travel around the world delivering lectures at universities or anything of the sort—no & I won't discover a new theory of physics. Used to think there wasn't a limit to what I was going to be, just as though I was 8 years old and believed I'd live forever. Now I know I'm stuck where I am, and I know I'm going to die. At times I lift my head & seem to be gasping for breath. Feel submerged in the life around me. If that's so—well, the core of my self-sufficiency is weakening. What would happen if I tattooed my face?

SEPTEMBER 13

Last night to the church but she wasn't there. I waited until the basement lights went out. How often I've waited. So much of life is Waiting. Localities, objects, circumstances leading up to—yes, that lead Up To. And there we're left, roads end at the cliff.

SEPTEMBER 14

Women betray us because they care for nothing except pleasure. So we become distraught & violent, seek opportunities to assault them. Also, because of the things they put on themselves. Silky veils. Buttons and tassels, fringes, articles of silk and rubber. Then their features become an abomination in the sight of Mankind. It is no wonder that Napoleon ordered young Viennese girls brought to his room at the castle, demanded they take off their clothes, then shouted at them that they were interrupting his work &

rushed off to confer with his officers. The gesture's appropriate. Appropriate is the word.

Have begun to feel more confident, more vigorous. The future doesn't appear so bleak. For once I've been honest, and being so once, why should I degenerate? I've been concerned by thoughts of failure and while despising myself how could I possibly hold others in much esteem? That's correct. The Self can disappear, being replaced by a moment of the highest satisfaction. They say that during the mating season, for example, the wild cock absolutely ignores the hunter. Death shrivels under the glorious light of Love. So it is.

Just now went up to the roof to enjoy the first bright autumn constellations.

SEPTEMBER 15

Finally I've realized what she wants, therefore why she did what she did. Not money because she's got that, what she wants is publicity. Millions of people to admire her. I don't know why I didn't realize this sooner. Now at least I thank God that my eyes have been opened! How vulgar she is, how cheap. How insignificant as compared to the majesty above our heads. It's painful to admit this because I actually did care for her. Maybe I loved her, maybe I did. But now it's plain she isn't worth five minutes of my love. I don't even like the shape of her nose, I never have. Her hair twisted up like a cocoon. Voice reminds me of buttermilk in a saucer. No, I don't like her. All this time I've wasted. She was an interruption—that's it. Nothing else. And I can honestly say I don't hate her for what she did to me. What I feel when I think about her is Indifference. That's all. I have complete lack of concern. Let her live, let her die, I don't care. Hours I wasted imagining how it would be to live with her, imagining a home and her as my wife. I can remember how often I spoke her name—Mara Summerfield. Thought it was so balanced! Just as if that proved we belonged together! Used to think I'd feel complete with her, instead of feeling like half of something. How little we know about ourselves! I thought how wonderful it would be to have children with her and make her happy for the rest of my life, etc. Well, now I know better & am thankful. I wouldn't lower myself.

Maybe I'm not everything I'd like to be or used to think I was going to be, but she's not much either. Treating me like dirt. But of course people would say I was in the wrong. Doesn't matter if she opened up quicker than the cheapest slut in the market—no matter, Summerfield's to blame.

So much for her, so much for me.

SEPTEMBER 16

Will get her on the phone in a little while. Think of what to ask. Ask about that movie contract, if she did everything they wanted her to do when she went down there. Also, warn her not to lie to me or else. Excited thinking about it—can't keep still. Out we come! How would she like to see That? Give her a taste of it. Oh yes, am going to ask about the movie contract, ask if those Hollywood big shots are coming up to get her. Going to suck them? Lie to me and you'll regret it, am warning you. She won't hang up because she loves to hear me say things like that. I know what she is.

194

SEPTEMBER 17

Past concerns of past days, agitation & desire. Fits of pique, frigid passions, nights ruined with a mummy hand, baffled by the beat of my own heart. So dreams turn to paper—dry as crumbled crackers! Beetle husks. Straws pulled out of worn brooms. Dust. Echoes. Sweepings of autumn.

Is it because I value so little?

SEPTEMBER 18

Vladimir told me a year or so ago that he used to live in a cottage in southern France near the border of Spain. Mas Audran—yes, that was the name of the place, stuck in my mind, near Lodeve in Heerold or Herault or some such. I remember that he said the cottage was in bad shape, nothing worked, no electric lights, and shutters dropping off the hinges. Wasn't even a pump, he had to get water from the stream. Why did he live there? Have forgotten, yet that's not important. He said the cottage was close to the edge of a cliff and he could look down on a valley filled with vineyards and an old Roman aqueduct, and he could see a hundred kilometers to the hills of Auvergne. It must have been at least two years ago he told me, might as well be yesterday. How often I've seen the place in my mind. I think I could find it. I sometimes think I could walk out of this apartment and go there by myself.

Of course, Earl. Ask Bianca for your freedom, give up your job at the Bureau and fly to Europe, to the south of France & live like a poet. Oh yes. Actually, what's going to happen? Tomorrow—wake up two seconds before the alarm goes off, sit on the side of the bed for a while wiping

195

your eyes and trying not to think. Unbutton your pajamas, take a piss and brush your teeth, comb your hair hoping no more of it falls out, shave, eat, ride downtown—oh my God my God. Is it so difficult to predict? Tomorrow joins tomorrow. Tomorrow & tomorrow & tomorrow!

SEPTEMBER 19

It'll be Christmas again before long. How fast a year goes. How little it contains. Christmas. No rose of such virtue as is the rose that bare Jesu. Alleluia! But what happened on earth this day? Another housewife died in some East Bay abortion mill. For in that rose was Heaven in little space. Res miranda! By that rose we may well see one God in Persons three. Angels sing & shepherds too—Gloria in excelsis Deo. Leave we all this worldly mirth & follow we this joyful birth. Leave we all this worldly mirth!

Oh, I guess our Christmas is going to be like any number of previous ones. Can visualize it now. It seems to promise, but so did the last as well as the one before. Usually the case, neither our brightest hopes nor darkest fears are met. Occasionally, though, I guess they are.

SEPTEMBER 20

Tinkle of glass somewhere down the street caused me to forget whatever was in mind but no matter. Presently I'll be taken with a new idea, hope it's going to be worthwhile. Soon my head's going to be full of popcorn. Very much the same. Indeed, my thoughts are weightless—as tough and white as popcorn. I could shower the earth with my thoughts.

SEPTEMBER

Turned off the light a minute ago but the moon is so bright I'm still able to write.

SEPTEMBER 21

Bianca told me tonight that beginning next semester she's going to be the school Vice-Principal. Learned about it several days ago but only tonight did she deign to let me know. Why? I've been here at the desk for three hours asking that question. The insult was deliberate. It proves exactly what she thinks of me. Lifted her eyebrows when I said "Thank you very much!" Since then not a word, obviously she's decided to avoid the subject. There used to be a time when she told me everything, no matter how trivial, but she's gotten conceited. I'm not good enough to meet her intellectual friends. Spach and his fat wife have been here often enough sipping coffee but does she ask me to join them? That history teacher and all the rest of their bunch— they remind me of pelicans! Well, I might tell her what I think one of these days.

Surrounded by them, it's natural to be entangled. I'm not going to deny the fact. Simply a matter of circumstance. What we do is as preordained as the pattern of a minuet.

It's begun to rain.

SEPTEMBER 22

Tried to speak civilly tonight, thought I'd make an honest attempt to compliment her on the promotion. She listened with a bored expression, then shook her head and thanked me at the same time! It occurred to me that she was asking me to kill her, squeeze the elements out of her throat.

197

I've thought of it but the fact is I don't actually dislike her that much. I believe when we first got married I could have —oh, it's hard to say. Hard to say.

Burn her clothes? Could do that. Idea keeps coming back, clinging to my scalp like a salt flake. Suppose I gathered up everything she owns and burnt it! For the first time in her life she'd be embarrassed.But I don't think I'll do it, much as I'd like to. No, it's a theatrical thought & I don't have time for that. Gestures and elaborate poses—nothing doing! Knots tighten while the year pulls in. Can't imagine where I'll be next September at this time, although of course it doesn't matter.

Sitting here asking myself a favorite question: Why did you get married to a woman with Paper Tubes? Don't know how often I've asked it, and go on reminding myself that my body knew hers was a joke. Nothing but straw inside. The body always knows. So why did I do it? Others are full of liquid. Ah well, done is done & I guess we pick out whatever we need. No sense throwing it in her face any more because she's gotten to the point where it's impossible to talk to her. Drifted beyond the reach of any sort of reasonable discussion. As for myself, solitude and work, obligated by Nature. Work and think and work again. At times I see Earl Summerfield as a dwarf, crafty old homunculus painting a fresco on a bloody wall—no, no, it's not as rigid as a wall. Appears to be the inner chamber of the heart.

So much for that! Yawning. Tomorrow's Monday. With this constant rain the Bureau's going to be crowded. I'd better get some sleep.

SEPTEMBER 23

Mr. Foxx is to be transferred, so McA claims— and not to a higher post. Hard to credit. McA could be wrong. Foxx is a decent person. Have never really believed those stories about him. He wouldn't degrade himself the way everybody else does. Stenos in his office but—yes, but what? WHAT?

The fact is I know he's guilty. Everybody knows. He's sacrificed his dignity for a few minutes of greasy satisfaction. All of us know. I'm the only one that kept pretending, hoping it wasn't true. Can't say why, unless it's because I needed somebody to look up to. I guess I see him now as he is. Truly as he is, neither better nor worse. I suppose all of us coarsen and harden imperceptibly, the inner light grows feeble, the soul's window narrows as the flesh loses its first firmness until at last we retain only the weight of our wrongdoing.

SEPTEMBER 24

Weather has finally cleared & clouds are floating east tonight. I spent quite a while on the roof with my telescope, otherwise didn't go out of the apartment, which surprised Bianca—I could feel her staring at me while I read the paper but why explain? Each time she was about to question me I cleared my throat. That puzzled her. However, she understood my mood. Being weaker than we are they've attuned themselves through thousands of generations to remain in harmony with us, knowing perfectly well that otherwise we'd destroy them.

Also, she must be afraid of me for a better reason—because I know as much as I do.

SEPTEMBER 25

Happened to meet Lundborg while waiting for my bus this morning. Hadn't seen him for almost a year consequently I asked where he'd been and he said that he'd been traveling. Suddenly came into my head to ask if he'd discovered the New Heaven and the New Earth, so that's what I did, and laughed so he'd know it was a joke, but he looked at me strangely. He seemed embarrassed, which made me angry—as though he was ashamed to know me. Said something I regret & shook my fist, which of course made the situation worse. People started whispering, etc., so I walked away. There wasn't much point trying to explain. Everything considered it was the start of a very unpleasant day what with Aneurine gazing at me and so forth. I shouldn't let such little things upset me, but no, I've got to hoard them. Collect and polish them as eagerly as Magnus polishing his bag of odd brass buttons, sort them & organize them in perfect rows, then rearrange them. It seems to me my brain's always trying to gather up elusive meanings but God alone knows why. Useless useless. Meanwhile the days wash in and out.

SEPTEMBER 26

Peter Brandt's been convicted. Death in the gas chamber, although I doubt if he's next. I think they've got a waiting list. Anyway, more or less to my surprise the city's divided—half of the people think he's getting what he deserves, the other half insisting he was framed. He's guilty, guilty, guilty as can be, I knew that right away and am puzzled that anybody'd want to defend him. Strange, remote as he is, judging from the latest picture. Sickly pale, looks like he's been eating candied fruit. Leans back in his chair and strokes his fingers, probably thinking about the good citizens who want to tear him to pieces, also about the ones that send him gifts. I guess he touched a public nerve. Mmm— yes, no doubt. That face, feminine fingers, soft moist affectionate eyes. Didn't hesitate to trade his life for half an hour of—well, of what? Not passion, he's too deep in the hole. Clammy, joyless greed, more like it. Makes me think of the Victorians, he'd feel at home with them. Yes, I know his attitude. Some participate, others don't. Look at him, serene & composed! Not the least bit worried about visiting our fresh little apple-green chamber, but why not? Why isn't he worried? Should be terrified, because that's what it's all about, oh but he isn't, not Peter Brandt. Oh no, and it makes the decent law-abiding citizens angry, bet on that. Yes, looking at his face must exasperate them. He ought to be trembling, praying, on his knees begging forgiveness. Ha! They're adding to his pleasure. Probably the only thing that upsets him is when he's misquoted, or when somebody takes an unflattering picture.

Well, Peter Brandt, sorry we're not going to meet. We're not the least alike but we'd get along. We'd understand each other. Or would you understand me? I can't be sure. Stagnant ponds, mossy waters. None of that for me. Could you ever understand how I felt? I'll tell you—I felt like one of those early Christians banging his sword against the walls of Antioch. And you, like some Oriental with a poisoned arrow. A Saracen in his tower. Ho! Not much of a surprise you won't beg for mercy. Anyway, we're not related, at least I don't think so. Different as different can be Mr. Brandt— snake from a bumblebee. We won't meet, not on earth, nor am I particularly sorry to see you go. What does annoy me, however, is the stupidity of certain people in the street. Let us have him! We'll teach the fiend a lesson! etc. etc. You & I know better, eh? Lessons are no more taught than learned.

201

SEPTEMBER 27

Considering my thoughts of last night, they sound confused. What was I talking about? And why should I care what becomes of Peter Brandt—he's a common sort, a Type. He's no more unique than a camel. He's anxious to be poisoned, society anxious to oblige. Let each smell the other's odor.

My hair keeps falling out. In certain lights anybody would think I was sixty. Bag developing beneath my chin. I think I eat too many sandwiches. Pies, cakes, not enough salad and fruit. Sitting all day doesn't help. I don't dare weigh myself.

Heigh-ho, an untidy week. I've fluttered back and forth from the apartment to the office, tried to liberate my soul but can't prove I've been successful. I've tried not to think about M. St. J. Attempting to discipline the mind. Have said to myself that the emotions of the senses do not satisfy us, as long as we are on earth we go in search of Heaven despite the knowledge that we'll never find it. Yet what's the use of moral attitudes?—I do come circling back to her & think of her just as steadily as a planet thinks of the sun. Bad luck, bad luck, misfortune for us both.

SEPTEMBER 28

Saturday and no better. If somebody asks me what she's like what could I say? Like so-and-so but of course very different. Umm, let me put it this way. She's like—well, do you understand? No. Then put it some other way. This or that. Nobody could understand. Of course she Is like the others, they're all alike. Haunches as large and solid as the paws of granite lions, yes, and give off an odor like a beach when the tide runs out & we go into them as eagerly as silverfish slip into the binding of a little book. All right, she's like the rest, she's like them but—why go on?

I guess I don't have much idea what to say. She was like a chord of music. Beyond that, I don't know. I'm so miserable. Could sit here in dust, darkness and ashes for the rest of my life.

SEPTEMBER 29

Was not able to control myself, I needed so much to hear her voice. Thought she might not recognize me, not with a handkerchief near my lips, but she began to cry and threaten me. Then suddenly she stopped, that was what made me suspicious. And with good reason. Somebody else was there because I heard whispering. Put me in an ugly temper so I said things I never meant to say. Sorry for what I said. I wanted us to have a nice conversation but I didn't know how to express the feeling in my heart.

SEPTEMBER 30

Another month concludes. Ninth of this terrible year. I feel as though I'm traveling down some desolate path between steep cliffs. Nobody to guide me but I go on walking, always descending.

OCTOBER 1

I used to believe we needed Love. Every living thing requires some sign of Love—that's what I believed, no longer. My own existence proves how false that is, I could go back eight years to list five people who were glad to see me. And as for the love between men & women—a myth. Nobody's certain what it is. They can't point to it any more definitely than they can point to the throne of God. Is it overhead? One authority clears the phlegm out of his throat, adjusts his spectacles and tells us the meaning of love, describes it as though it was an elephant's ear. Then the next authority tells us it's more in the nature of a rope, the elephant's trunk. Etc. etc. But I say it doesn't exist. Do I feel a sense of love for Bianca? No. What I feel for her is a form of loathing, as though she was contaminated. If I had a different feeling for her several years ago what was that? Was that Love? I doubt it. I felt something larger than affection, yes, and what became of it? Was I deceived then, or am I now? Tricked twice? Or say that I did know what it meant to love somebody but don't any longer? If that's the case when did my understanding disappear? Love is a wine that turns to vinegar. But who am I to have opinions? I've never accomplished anything. Conceited, treacherous little bureaucrat, cowardly and vain. I could go on describing myself—useless. I do have good points. Sensitive and intelligent, yes, no doubt of that! It's just that I never had an opportunity to distinguish myself. Partly that's my own fault because I dream too much, do too little, but also circumstances have been against me. Forced to work every day at a job that doesn't challenge me. Waste! Waste! Millions in my position, some of them rise above it. Why can't I? Well, I'd rather think about achieving something than setting down to work at it. Right now I ought to be studying physics or—well, whatever. Maybe I should get into politics. My name somehow has a political sound. Earl Summerfield. Assemblyman Summerfield, 9th district. Comptroller, yes, or even a legal position. Attorney General Summerfield this morning conferred with officials of so forth & so on. His wife, Bianca, Superintendent of Schools, etc. Yes, contemplate what you might have been instead of what you are. And night after night you sit here dreaming your life away.

B rattling the knob, pounding on the door. I suppose I've got to answer. All right, put the journal out of sight. Yes, Bianca, one moment. If only she could see me now—wagging it at her. That's how I respond to threats.

OCTOBER 2

B suspicious, wants to know if I'm spending money. Why is the account so low? I knew she was going to discover it but hadn't expected an argument so soon. Well, not an argument, since I didn't speak. Part of the money's mine so why doesn't she let me do as I please with it? On the other hand I see why she's disturbed. Of course she always worries about money. Both of us work hard. However I'm puzzled that she didn't keep on questioning me, usually she does. I have a feeling she knew I was about to answer and she was afraid to hear what I was going to say. She doesn't want to know where the money went. She'll try to figure it out, though, I know her well enough to know that. Pretend I've started drinking after work? No, she wouldn't believe that. Also, if I really was drinking she'd know I'd try to hide the fact. Could pretend to be concealing it? No—she'd soon pick that apart, she's too clever to be deceived. Why hasn't she ever trusted me? From the first day we saw each other I suspected she didn't entirely trust me. I wonder how life would have been for the two of us if she'd had more faith.

Stirring my finger through the past. Muddy leaves.

OCTOBER 3

It must be the appointment that's made B so officious recently. Speaks to me as though I was a child. Yes, exactly, she makes me feel like one of her students. Knocked at the bedroom door. "What do you want Earl? I'm reading." Asked if I could come in, thought we might have a talk, then she wants to know what about, repeats that she's reading. Obviously doesn't want to be bothered. Then in that very bored voice tells me the door is open. I wonder how long I'd been standing in the hall—5 minutes? At least, maybe longer. There she was propped up in bed thumbing through one of those books on how to make a fortune. Green towel around her head like a turban. I could smell the shampoo. Made a face but it didn't amuse her, she just lay there waiting. She didn't even think enough of me to close the book. Gazing at me over the top of those terrible glasses. For once in my life I didn't wait for her to attack but demanded sarcastically what she'd accomplished. Continued to stare at me as though dumbfounded & then all at once opened her mouth and coughed. Room full of cigarette smoke. I hadn't noticed it until she coughed. The air was gray, layers of smoke floating above the lamp. Maybe she'll fall asleep and burn to death. She's envious of me but refuses to admit it. I suppose she envies my intelligence. She seems to sense that the patterns of my brain are much too intricate for her to follow. Oh, she's intelligent enough herself, I don't deny that, but she hardly compares with me. She merely commits to memory the best ideas of far more subtle minds. She's smart enough to acknowledge this. I'll say that much for her. Otherwise there's no comparison and I can tell the contempt she shows me is a mask for admiration. Well, I left her with a few things to think about. Simply turned my back on her & marched out, stiff as a soldier. Let her puzzle over the situation, it might do her some good. She's not a woman anyway, her body's practically vaporized. No more of those early visceral humors, she's not recognizable any longer. Not a woman. Dust & dry webs.

All right Earl, stop pitying yourself. Happiness was never certain, considering the obstacles. Paradise is the place where you live on roasted apples, not on this earth, not till you hear the blast of the Trumpet and become aware of the steady click of the universe.

Very familiar sensation—as though I was a prism through which rays of light are flowing. Colors. Marvelous colors! Also, right here on earth my stomach's growling! Didn't want supper but now I think I'll go into the kitchen and gobble up a chicken leg.

OCTOBER 4

Last night while eating I became aware of the electric clock humming & stood watching the red pointer sweep around the dial. Felt very sad, although I don't know why. Thought of the house where I grew up and realized for the first time that it was a dead house. All those years I lived there it didn't occur to me. At the table we didn't discuss anything, just ate our food and went away. Was never any music, not at the table or before or afterward. Once a year, at Christmas, Aunt Ollie put carols on the phonograph. Also, no birds or fish—there was a dog once, that was all. No plants in the house—wrong, in the alcove I remember some sort of a vine, although it never flowered. I don't know what it was. Leaves would turn brown and drop on the floor, it went on living by itself. And I don't think anybody knew the house was dead, they just used it. I guess what I'll never forget is the fact there wasn't any music. I wonder if it matters. To live year after year like that. Death in life. No, I exaggerate as usual. Have always been a Romantic.

OCTOBER 5

Bianca asked about the money. Ran out of the apartment and to a movie but hardly saw what it was. Sat in the darkness with fists clenched until confidence returned. Thought she'd be asleep when I got in but she heard me open the door, now she's lying in there awake. How much does she suspect? Anyway, I can't talk to her, can barely open my mouth. Jaws have been locked for an hour. It feels like my teeth are bending out of their sockets.

OCTOBER 6

Sunday. Had difficulty waking up this morning. My head felt porous. Sat on the edge of the bed blinking and fingering my skull. Impression of sand dropping on my shoulders, also was terribly frightened that my head was gradually turning to limestone. Called Bianca and seeing her was reassuring except for the radiance of her skin. Felt exhausted by the effort of staring at her. I wanted her to stay with me but she went out. Nothing came of it—I'm all right now. It was some sort of nightmare. But still whenever I think about this morning I grow uneasy.

Nothing to be concerned about. Tension of work and of course the horrifying things that happen every day. People inform each other with strange messages. Slashing. Burning. Stealing from the blind. Right up the ladder to the top where maniacs sit behind walnut desks & issue mad Announcements. In the name of reason, yes, pounce on curious enemies. Kill. Bomb. Murder.

Blood, bone & feathers. Whatever happens must happen in accord with a vast design.

OCTOBER 7

Being latest in the sequence of evolution it follows that Man must be the least perfect form of life.

OCTOBER 8

Drusilla Gorette, age 12, disappeared late yesterday after parents sent her to the dime store to buy a spool of thread. This noon two workmen sat down on a heap of shingles to eat their lunch, one noticed a little foot protruding & so they found Drusilla. At least they found most of her. The head and a few fingers still are missing.

OCTOBER 9

Wednesday. Further confirmation. Vincent di Georgio, aged 83, made the mistake of walking home from his office late last night instead of taking the taxi as he usually did. This A.M. his corpse turned up in the fountain at the civic center. Meanwhile on the other side of Market Street the body of an unidentified man about 40 years old was discovered in a hotel room near the YMCA, his hands and feet tied with silk scarves & his mouth clogged with toilet paper. Some fairly funny business there, at least that's my opinion. What will tomorrow bring? I ask & ask again. But of course it's easy to guess—another deposit of silt. Generation after generation.

Whoever tries to bring mankind back to his senses either through the use of reason or by other methods must be deluded. I see that now. Terrors of the world do not become less frequent, just the opposite. Tomorrow will be worse, I could easily paint a picture of tomorrow. Mounds of human excrement. Priests from every nation holding up red chalices brimming with urine. Yet at the same time we sing of charity & we sing of peace, ad infinitum!—until the mountains of Tibet echo back our canticle of Brotherhood. Nobody believes it, least of all those that sing the loudest. Transeamus. Gaudeamus. Pari forma. Res miranda. Yet who am I to criticize? Who am I?

OCTOBER 10

Out for a stroll last night and took along the umbrella although the sky was clear. Just thought I might need it, and as usual I was right. Not sure quite what happened. I do remember some woman approaching, next I heard a few screams & there I was running lightly away. It was very much like a dream. Perhaps that's all it was, there's nothing in the Chronicle. Hmm, probably I fell asleep. Well, there's no need to be concerned. The divagations of the heart transcend the mind, and Truth's a thing we can appreciate from numerous points of view as though it was a—what's the word I want? Somehow quite degrading not to produce the word when needed. Nearly through an elegant dance and can't think where to put your foot. Ah well, Earl, be thankful you're as brilliant as you are.

OCTOBER 11

Wakening more and more slowly each morning & lie in a half-dream of what I could accomplish. They say daydreaming is the prelude to each great & imaginative achievement. The fantasies of Man must be bold and creative if they are to spark the highest energies within. It's the daydream that inspires us. Eventually, I think, we'll prove capable of achieving whatever we have the power to imagine. True. True.

OCTOBER 12

Opening the door when I came home this evening I almost staggered—stretched out my hands, shut both eyes & held my breath. That's how the place affects me. I've walked through the door too often, it's as simple as That. I know that walking through the same door thousands of times is a symbol of madness. What this means to me is that I've got to get away, soon. Soon. I can't stay here. I can't sit here many more nights turning over my past as though it was a handful of tarnished pennies. Traveling could save me. If I traveled East to a domed city where the doors and windows are covered with striped awnings, roads are narrow, white doves flutter in the sunlight and cool water plays against the noonday heat. If I could smell camels & goats & sandalwood, cooking oil, incense, aromatic herbs smoldering in metal braziers. Persian carpets on the wall, painted ceilings and inlaid tiles and colored mosaic, copper dishes, ivory boxes, almond paste, women in white muslin. If I was there I'd soon be feeling much much better, I'm positive. The trouble is that I've denied myself all the things I've wanted, concentrating my sensibilities upon the life around me. A mistake that could be fatal. Already it's gotten so bad I dance around the room shaking my fists.

Perhaps I actually could take a trip. But on the other hand—well, I just don't know. I can't decide. It's seldom now that I can say what I might or might not do.

OCTOBER 13

Occurs to me I'm like a bird that darts down a chimney into somebody's house & once inside dashes itself to death against a window. Unable to distinguish invisible Obstacles.

OCTOBER 14

Pigeons stand attentively on the ledge, quiet as gargoyles from Krakow. Judging me, I think. Life so far is a solemn wait from birth to death. It's a farce badly contrived & weakly acted. The flesh a palimpsest of lies.

OCTOBER 15

Mercy. Mercy on Earl Summerfield.

OCTOBER 16

Too much time peeping toward life, that's why I've lost the power to love. If I ever had it. How can I be sure? All I know is that the sight of love is more real to me than reality. Moving skin, warm hands—gone, gone like a swarm of wings! I sit here coldly gnawing my fingertips and wonder if it's too late. Doubt if that's possible, I've come this far. The fact is, Earl Summerfield, you're damned.

But still our senses often deceive us. How many times I've supposed that a thing must be so when really it's not. Also, at such times I had no way of knowing I'd been deceived. Therefore it's possible that at any moment I'm being deceived. All of us duped as easily as children out of school.

I can't write any more, not tonight. My head rings back & forth. Tom o'Bedlam's song.

OCTOBER 17

Money to my queen again.

OCTOBER 18

Some kind of rhythm has settled in me & I can't stop, can't prevent myself. I think I've escaped but then I know I'm caught. She's gotten underneath me like a succubus. Without her I'll milk myself to death.

OCTOBER 19

Saturday. Wandered through the Tenderloin this evening about dusk. Women sidling out of restaurants & out of hotels, beckoning, whispering. If it wasn't for them I believe I'd be at peace with the universe, the sight of them turns my blood to pus. They suck us down and they swallow us in spite of our protests. Filthier than pigeons that fluff & squat on rooftops. Rotting bulbs cast up by the sea. Murmuring, gathering things around them. It's the mindless lethargy of their motions that I hate. Lotions, creams, spit on their red mouths. I told them to leave me alone. I showed them all the palm of my hand, and washed myself from head to foot as soon as I got home but somehow I still don't feel clean. If I could just forget them, I know their lives aren't worth five minutes of my thought.

OCTOBER 20

This A.M. outside Unity Presbyterian. Gazed at the passers-by but none recognized me. Obviously I don't mean much. Walked inside, stood awhile listening to the minister. Dust motes settling through a beam of light. Polished wood & leaded glass. His sermon had to do with the fifteenth chapter of Luke, which speaks of wasting one's Substance. Certainly this applies to me.

Looked for M. St. J. in the congregation and in the choir. Looked and looked. No luck. So mark the end of Sunday.

OCTOBER 21

Industry and Virtue shall be rewarded, saith the Preacher. Yes, that's what I believed. I accepted these so-called truths but I know better now. This Monday taught me quite a lot. McAuliffe's been promoted. Month after month I worked harder than he did and statistics bear me out, not the slightest doubt. I don't need to see Aneurine's little chart. I know & everybody in the department knows he does less work than anybody else, also that I do more. But he's charming, doesn't hesitate to manipulate things or people if they can do him some good. Well, he told me a long time ago that the Bureau doesn't care how hard you work, you won't get anything for it. I told him that wasn't the case. Told him that industry and virtue sooner or later have got to be rewarded & he grinned. But he was right. I've been a simple fool. Not a day's gone by when I didn't glance at old Clegg and think to myself it won't happen to me. I won't sit in the same place until I collapse and die. Not I. Oh no, not Earl Summerfield! Thirty years from now toppling off of my stool, then somebody brings a blanket out of a closet somewhere and everything's over. Isn't going to happen to me. Oh no?

Ideas about Self-Fulfillment used to occupy me, but now I recognize how that degrades us. New insight begins only when possibilities of achieving satisfaction have disappeared forever, when everything that's been said, seen & done shows itself as Distortion.

Starting to feel as I did many years ago when I recognized my face in a mirror for the first time. I knew then that I actually existed. Earl Summerfield was alive on earth—what a discovery! Now I discover I'm here for no particular purpose. Used to imagine my greatness & my success.

THE DIARY OF A RAPIST

Imagined the time I'd get aboard a famous ocean liner while photographers gathered around me, on my way to the estate of some Scottish nobleman, for example, traveling with a beautiful actress or a bunch of rich Greeks. Or discussing various important matters aboard somebody's yacht in the Mediterranean. Thought it was going to happen.

We enter the world on a shower of stars but how does it end? Ho ho ho.

OCTOBER 22

Names & places change but that's all. Early this morning some cocktail waitress in Fillmore district was kidnaped and screwed by a bunch of Negroes. Doubt if it's the first time, of course it's not the last. Next year, last year, what's the difference? Police have caught 5 of them and expect to pick up a few more. Victim in the hospital in serious condition, not able to say exactly how many there were. Suppose they catch a dozen, all get the Death Penalty! Hmm. Disagreeable to have so many executions. Two or three without much of a fuss, easy to forget, but a dozen! Would be like Roman times. But suppose. All right. Gas chamber seats 2, after which it takes a while to air the place and clean up the mess. Vomit, urine, pus, etc. before the next pair can be seated. Might take a full day to kill a dozen. And of course what if there were 15 or 20? Well, it's interesting to think about. Maybe the problem could be solved by getting rid of them graually over a period of months, a couple at a time, avoid publicity. Some sort of legal hocuspocus, could be arranged. Well, it's what we deserve. Remember reading about certain eels that swim thousands of miles in order to lay their eggs on the floor of the Sargasso Sea, then later the eggs float to the surface and drift right back where they belong, nobody knows why. Spawn of a

216

nation mysteriously comes drifting back. Always has, always will.

Yawning. Can't keep my eyes open. A good rest is what I need. Don't think I'll write any longer, have no worthwhile thoughts. Go for a long walk tomorrow night, study the city.

Can't quit yawning.

OCTOBER 23

Whatever you may be, or may not, Earl Summerfield, you're clever. By the time they traced the call you'd drifted out of sight as calmly as an eel's egg. And if they do locate the booth they won't find any prints. Nothing but somebody's odor. Yes, as careful as I'm clever—why pretend I'm not? Abusing myself so often, heaping such blame on myself, I might as well accept a little credit. I may be sick of what I do—and I am, yes, I am, I'd give anything to stop —but constantly accusing myself's no help. After all, I'm not guilty. Next year perhaps—BZZZT! and Summerfield becomes an altogether different man. If that's possible, how can I be blamed? Can't. In fact, if that's possible not one of us means a thing! Napoleon becomes a clerk, etc. Therefore why should I despise this weakness? And yet I do. I wonder why that is. Promising to improve, then weakening, overcome by the river rising up inside. That's always how it is. The last thing I remember was a siren & red lights flashing, next I was in that booth reaching up to unscrew the light. Squeezing the flag while I made my call. But it was cold pleasure, I want more than a frightened voice. What I want is her soul. Well, is there any hope? Was she glad to hear from me again? I guess not. The things I said I didn't mean. Shouting, trembling, all because—well, because of her fiancée. I'd kill him if I had a chance. I've never hated anybody half as much. Just the same I ought to control my temper.

217

Acting as I do, of course she doesn't want to talk. Teeth clenched, words pouring out—three times since July & each call unsatisfactory. If only I could be pleasant. I'll try again before long. I'm anxious for her to like me.

Just now occurs to me that maybe it would be a good idea to let her know who I am, at least tell her a few interesting things about me. Where I work. Say I'm married but have no children. Ask if she wants children. Let her know I think about her day & night. The body turns to ashes, in time our names are going to be forgotten and people won't remember who we were. Yes, that's what I'll say to her the next time I call. It explains just how I feel.

So much for that! Tomorrow's Thursday. Rain forecast. If so the office will be crowded. I'd better try once more to get some sleep.

OCTOBER 24

Unable to close my eyes last night. Left the apartment this A.M. before dawn and walked to the Bureau—five miles, six miles. Climbed over fences, walked through vacant lots getting my hands dirty, mud on my shoes, also a scratch on my cheek from pushing through some shrubbery. A few minutes late to work. Aneurine and Fensdeicke both stared at me. In fact almost everybody did, not without reason. It was foolish of me. Explained to Fensdeicke that I hadn't been able to sleep so had decided to walk to the office but it took longer than I expected and I was trying to save time by taking shortcuts. Everything just as it actually happened. She didn't say a word but she looked at the clock again to make sure I understood that I was late. So washed my face & hands, straightened my tie, put in the usual day and after a while nobody paid much attention.

OCTOBER

Rain again is forecast. It didn't materialize today and somehow I doubt it will tomorrow. I like dry weather.

OCTOBER 25

Sleep's approaching. I welcome it & yet I'm afraid. I might have a dream, which is what I want, but asleep I won't be able to direct it. Maybe by drawing pictures I can keep awake. Maybe not. Suppose that I was to draw a picture but then burn it. Bianca would certainly wake up, I know she can smell things in the middle of the night. If I wanted to burn it I'd be forced to hold it outside the window, even then I'd be afraid she'd rap at the door. "Earl, what are you doing? For the love of God—" What does she know of God? A cloak to conceal the void. That's usually the way, those who understand least are first to speak. Suppose I let her know I was burning a scrap of paper, open the door a crack to show her the ashes. She wouldn't be amused. How would she respond? I wonder if that would be enough to make her lose patience. If I deliberately burned something else, and then something else, how long before she'd get really angry with me? Also, what would she do once I'd made her furious?

OCTOBER 26

Sickened by my own plans & amazed at how they form, bubbles on the surface of a marsh. Attempts at discipline worse than useless—impelled to shameful acts despite myself. As though I was some sort of creature that avoids the light! Under a tree in the park this afternoon, jacket buttoned to my neck and cap down over my face so that nobody would dare speak to me. Children playing with a ball, lovers wandering about while I could think of nothing except my filthy need. I'm sick of my own presence, revolted by everything that's ever gone through my head. Vile words drop from my lips of their own accord—I get dizzy thinking about them, yet worse is my cowardice. People suspect how cowardly I am, forcing me to take some weak revenge in secret. Each act insists upon another. When will it stop? Yesterday told Vladimir I'd welcome being locked up in prison because there at least I'd have a sense of freedom. I'm not sure he understood but it's plain enough—how pleasant life must be when you know what you're privileged to do and what you're not. Prisoners must be very much at ease. I envy them, I'd welcome twenty years of prison life. V thought that was curious. He says just the idea of being jailed is enough to drive him mad. Does it matter whether the bolt's inside or out? That's what I ought to ask, find out if he can answer. Next I'll ask him what he thinks about my future. What have I to look forward to? Maybe he knows, I don't. These last few months I've seen the obvious facts. Admit I deserve nothing. Some do, others don't. McAuliffe doesn't deserve any rewards whereas Bianca does. Yes, I admit she does, I'll give her that much. She arranges situations so carefully, subtly, in fact quite ceremoniously that she ought to be rewarded. I have no doubt she will be, consequently it's not surprising how she treats me. She's ashamed of being married to me. I don't blame her. I'm less than Nothing. Contemptible. My tongue's as flat as a knife, lips smeared with scum. And of course the discrepancy between us will grow more obvious. Oh yes, my wife's certainly going to become important but I'm not. Nobody's fault, just a fact. I don't resent it. Certain trees grow higher than others, that's all. Really I don't resent McA, not any more. His taking advantage of me—oh I used to. I can remember when I hated him for cheating me out of the

220

money, yes, and imagined breaking into his apartment to destroy everything he owned because I thought that would serve him right for what he'd done to me. Now it seems impossible. Looked up his address, went out there and walked around the building planning how to get in. Now I accept his miserable swindling nature. He's what he is, he's not responsible any more than I'm responsible for what I am, and he'll always cheat whoever's ready to be cheated. Of course Foxx, Aneurine, Fensdeicke and the others who promoted him are stupid—he deceived them just as he deceived me, simple as that. He knows how to pull the handles, he knows how to operate the world, I don't. I never have known how it's done. Get other people to do the work you're supposed to do, accept the credit, shift blame. I guess finally the people I despise aren't the cheap small people like him but the ones who promote him. It's they who are responsible for holding me down. They can't see that I've always done the work. I've worked four times harder than McAuliffe. He's promoted. What's my future? Nothing. Why should I care what becomes of me? Let the State do as it pleases. Read those accounts in the paper, hear about it on radio, etc., but it's unreal. Peter Brandt's going to be killed and is anticipating the day, I think. Yes, I think he looks forward to the morning when he puts on those felt slippers, fresh blue denim trousers and a crisp white shirt. Be nicely dressed for the official audience. Well, to each his own. So far as I'm concerned the ceremony's a farce & the gas chamber's no more threatening than a brass wolf. Suspect everybody feels the same. Practically everybody, provided they think about it. But of course if Mr. Brandt wants to put on a show for us, be the center of attention for once, well, his own business. Blessings on them both, the Sacrifice and the State. Try to imagine it happening to me but that's impossible. Impossible. I just can't see myself as the victim. No, it's just not possible. Suppose it did happen to me, doubt if I'd be much upset. In that case, if I'm not concerned—not alarmed by the idea of being miserably put to death by that assembly of pious imbeciles why be frightened of Anything? A good question. Also, can't answer it, because I'm not only afraid this very minute, I've always been afraid. All my life, one thing or another. Cowardice is part of me—trickles through me like a vein of green blood, which is why the shameful words come pouring out & everything I ever touched started to decay. I'd give anything to be brave. However, I'm not. No help for it. At this moment there's nothing on earth I want more than to tell her who I am, reveal myself to her— everything I am & all I'm not. I want to tell her how I'm always thinking about her, but can't do it because I'm afraid. Pfut!

OCTOBER 27

Sunday. The sky is overcast. Winter's gathering high above. Days shorten, dances draw to a close.

Abjuring the past won't help—I'm simple as a child if I think so. The past is never with us, yet never apart. On & on it goes, describing the terrible figures of our future.

OCTOBER 28

Recently taken to counting. Toward what? There are 64 days left but why be concerned? What worries me? Only a sense that I won't succeed. Something will go wrong as it always does. Right now have difficulty breathing but that's because I'm Inside too much. Who else has lived in a world of wood lice & spider eggs?

Went up to the roof a few minutes ago with my telescope,

but there wasn't much to see. The wind blows from the north tonight and I doubt if our Lord is wakeful.

OCTOBER 29

If I reject Illusion—not forgetting it isn't Love to love only what resembles myself since that means loving nothing except myself—if I can remember that I can remember that what IS will always be. Sickness, age, death, but also a number of other things. Yes, if so, there won't be much to worry about. This year is soon going to be over. Days pass by majestically—huge white pelicans sculling along the beach. Nights are lost in the trough of a wave.

All right, soon the year does end. Whatever happens from now on I'll accept as my responsibility. That's not much, but without it we're finally corrupt.

OCTOBER 30

There must be aspects of our nature that neither Faust nor the Devil could foresee.

OCTOBER 31

This day wondering if I shall join the early Saints.

223

NOVEMBER 1

Ideally, I think, life ought to be severe & chaste. Have I myself attempted to live that way? I believe so. Example to be followed, discipline beyond the reach of most. Yes. Yes. Austerity and temperance. Integrity. Counter the evil tendencies of Man just as sailors counter currents driving them toward the Reef, thus the expression of attitudes impossible to those of lower sensibility. Object to object. Tincture of earthworm, poultice of adder's flesh.

NOVEMBER 2

Life is principally a matter of circumstance.

NOVEMBER 3

Have been thinking that I ought to burn the scrapbook—it's become apparent to me how notes & pictures lead us Downward. Certainly nobody would pretend that life's a thing to cut and paste. Nature creates us to take satisfaction where it's found. Indeed this must be the highest principle & goal of all existence.

224

NOVEMBER 4

Spending much time on the problem of Privacy. Privacy to meditate. Nothing's more important than discovering the center, without it there can't be any Sense to life. Withdraw and be utterly quiet in order to hear. Solitude a necessary protection. Invasions & wild alarms of society, period of time necessary for cure and recovery to health. Yes, that's so, despite the fact we're never alone, not even in seclusion. At any rate I'm convinced that before much longer I'll find myself miraculously freed from the miseries afflicting Mankind.

NOVEMBER 5

Last night dropped off to sleep at the desk. Dreamed I was dressed in ermine and velvet and was attending a masked ball. A foreign queen made advances to me, but I fled. Can't guess what this means. Intricate cloths our physicians weave are destined to be worn some other time.

Is this Tuesday or Wednesday? Flickety-flick!

Useless Earl. The wheel will turn whether you like it or not. Smile and sing alone. Messengers with tidings from the unknown skies greet you as you speed along the road.

NOVEMBER 6

Talking to Clegg during lunch, told me he and his wife awakened the other night by somebody pounding at their door. They lay in bed listening till it stopped, then went downstairs for a look and found a pool of blood on the doorstep. Nothing else. A pool of blood at the front door. I keep thinking about this and have an urge to get up, open my window, jump off the ledge and go sailing around San Francisco squawking like a parrot. Settle on fences squawking, eat some garbage, pull out tufts of my hair and eat that also. Why not? I could do it.

Have come to the conclusion that our parts govern us separately, like those snakes that climb around the staff of the medical emblem. Distinction between body & brain, or perhaps not. I don't know. Anyway, I've filled an envelope with fingernail clippings to represent the problems of the age.

NOVEMBER 7

Certain days I think about absolutely nothing except love, so then I can't feel much anger. None, in fact. Maybe it's the season, a time of year, or some inner change— who knows? Most people being just the opposite occupy themselves interminably with possibilities for revenge. Why is that? Because of the humiliations they have suffered. Thus the incessant degradation of others, instruments of torture.

Love and torture—oh yes! how tight we're bound. Gilles— mmm whatever-his-name, that marshal of France, worshiping Joan of Arc. Careful incision at the base of the neck, bodies gradually stiffening. Which is most beautiful? Which body? Children of France have a song that goes tum-tum-te-tum—nightingale sings its lovely tender melody in the wood because Gilles is dead—Gilles de Rais—there! Gilles de Rais is dead and Bluebeard is no more! How little they know. How little the children know.

Washed my face again but nothing helps. I can't eat, although my stomach's empty. Feeling faint & wan as moonlight on the water—I've got to get out of this room, visit strange houses. Not that I want to, I ought to stay here, but can't resist. Full as a jug with fluids of life. Movement beats against me & throws me down. As soon as B's asleep I'll go.

NOVEMBER 8

How very different I feel this evening! Now the wind as it sweeps through the park has another sound & it seems to me that all of us are preoccupied with imaginary crimes—incest, adultery, bigamy, etc. What a continuous list! Brutality's worse, yet somehow we honor that. Well, tweedle-dum, eh? Perhaps I'm much too harsh. I'd be a remorseless judge, have always been quite critical, yes, injustices 4 centuries old retain the power to infuriate me. I think about Galileo condemned by the Church of Rome and I clench my fists. Why? Isn't it finished? What's left for me to resent? Firing bullets at the sea, that's what you're doing. Put on a coal-black crown, knock at the door of the parish church, will you find a representative of God? Not exactly. Every time the same. What have I found? Doors that were locked, doors unlocked, but not once have I met with a powerful intellect. Nor did I see the mark of sensibility. I saw men wearing gowns dyed different colors but not one of them could bring a squirrel down from its tree unless he used a weapon. I asked myself what such men could teach me & got no answer, so I went away. I knew they were looking after me wondering what was wrong. I knew they must be wondering what I wanted, why I failed to speak, but how could my disappointment be explained? The moods of the heart in union or in separation exceed the limits of their belief. What have such men in common with St. Bernard who covered his eyes to avoid seeing the lakes of Switzerland?

227

THE DIARY OF A RAPIST

NOVEMBER 9

Disparate tendencies complement each other, have their own community. Yes, and what's most reasonable most disturbs the mad solicitation of Authority—reason, they answer, reason has the color of heresy, reason enough to doubt.

NOVEMBER 10

So, Earl, another week has ended. You survived, be thankful. The shadow of the eucalyptus drifts north, the city of San Francisco stinks with vice. Hypocrisy. Theft & Lies. Hail to the hieroglyph, to the sound of tramping boots. Buildings fall, wild screams, the clanking of religious armor. Could anybody suppose He labored six days to create This! My mother's labor was more profound.

Ask. Ask if life's always been like this. Or are we born in an age when the nature of God is changing?

NOVEMBER 11

Fee-fie-fo-fum. Holiday for Dead Soldiers. Now maybe I should have gone into military service. Certain I'd get along. Captain Summerfield. Major Summerfield. Kill. Missile. Gas attack. Destroy. Cleanse Evil.

NOVEMBER 12

Rather nice to escape from the office yesterday. So cool & bright that I walked all the way to Golden Gate

228

Park. Visited the aquarium, wildlife museum, across to the gallery, then to the Japanese tea garden where I ate some cookies, bought a postcard. Let's see, after that. To the flower conservatory. Hadn't been there in years, forgot how humid & sticky it is inside, gardeners constantly spraying those plants, puddles of water everywhere. Strange light filtering through that old glass, expected to meet people dressed in clothing from the Victorian era. Those little sticks with Latin names, smell of damp earth, etc. And next—oh! to the lake and rented one of those watercycles for an hour, pedaled around the island. I believe I'll do that again. Maybe take a bicycle ride through the park next time I have a day off. Next Saturday or Sunday, perhaps. Hmm. Excited by the flowers and those girls at the entrance, chased a peacock around a bush thinking I'd collect a few feathers with the idea of mailing them to my queen. Children laughed & pointed, noticed their parents looked uneasy, so hurried through the trees to another spot. However, I knew nobody would stop me—in fact I doubt if anybody reported me, it's too embarrassing. Call a policeman & try to explain what you've seen and why you're reporting it, how much simpler to ignore the situation. Yes, that amuses me. Like McAuliffe am learning to manipulate the world. Soon I'll know what people will do as well as what they won't. So perhaps I've not been wasting time. All the same it's fortunate I'm not impetuous, otherwise no telling. Lack of judgment—trouble, trouble.

Four in the morning! Should feel sleepy but I don't. Notice that I'm sleeping less than I used to, a few hours is enough whereas I used to need 9 or 10. Catnaps, up most of the night while Bianca lies dead as a toad. Hours of freedom while others sleep. Hours to walk about, examine alleys and garages, vault fences, climb into open windows, touch & smell, sample the food, look at the sleeping mummies. Listen to them breathe. I've touched their blankets. Last week

229

in that green apartment I thought I was going to faint. I left a fragrant present, yes, but did they understand? I hope they were impressed. At any rate, whatever I've done has been appropriate.

Light above the hills. Music on a distant radio.

NOVEMBER 13

Took a nap after getting home from work, then washed my hair, farted & made a few faces, studied my profile. I think I ought to lose a few pounds, even my shirt feels tight. Perhaps have been rewarding myself too often.

Yesterday's note makes little sense. Clear as a cheap snapshot & just about as meaningless. I mean to cure myself of—well, of what? Of what, Earl Summerfield! Nonessentials. Hours diddled away. Find the Kingdom of Heaven. Discover the key to the lock. But I see what happens every day and can't help feeling bitterly discouraged. Was it for This that a man was hung on a cross, Buddha traveled & Mohammed swayed along on a camel's back hour after hour beneath the desert sun? I can't believe it. To believe so I'd have to be mad, and knowing I'm as sane as other men becomes a penalty. Perhaps the smartest thing to do would be to sit in the garden all day like a bearded Indian, permit the heart to flow outward. Learn to say that because I've loved this life I must love death as well.

NOVEMBER 14

One more Thursday, how long since I've mentioned her? I told myself that if I was careful not to write her name I'd avoid temptation. It isn't so. Months have passed but the doubt's not resolved. She closed around me like a glove, I can't forget. At least not yet. Wobbling through each day wishing she was my wife—might as well admit it. I blame her for what happened, I feel no sense of guilt. Want her to admire me, still I'm disgusted by what she's done— thinking of how clumsily she struggled & the mindless stupefaction of her gaze. No more expression than a plastic doll —yes, that look of bland stupidity makes me furious. I've noticed it in others. Secret prompting of the senses but little else! Apparently it's enough for them to recreate themselves. They might as well be snails. Renewing themselves physically, not as we do. Love's all they comprehend. I remember there was a moment when I was going to speak but she pressed her thumb against my lips. Oh, the slightest movements tell the most! Who wouldn't despise her!

I believe she knew who I was. I'm sure she remembered me. She knows. Or maybe she thought the Devil rammed an icicle into her bloody rump. After all, why not? Who except a witch would kneel behind a church? That's right. Yes. She'd give herself to goats and donkeys. Christ, if I haven't realized until this instant what she is, what all of them are— maggots clustered in the soul of Mankind!

NOVEMBER 15

If I knew what she thought of me. Or if she's forgotten I exist. Am I a ghost? No. No, if I believed that I'd get rid of myself.

Maybe I could wrap up the shoe and send it back. She might want to wear it to remind herself. And then too, of course, being honest about the situation, sooner or later B's going to find my package, God above knows what would happen after That. Pays to be careful. Furthermore—ech ech, have lost my thought. Examining the shoe last night, yes, but then what? Was thinking also about tomorrow be-

THE DIARY OF A RAPIST

ing Saturday. Won't return, what's gone is gone. Lost in the crevices of my brain.

Early in the evening, earlier than I realized. Ask Bianca to go dancing? It's been a long time since we went anywhere together. Long long long time. And what she complains about is true—I hardly speak. I admit it, yes, these last few weeks or so I haven't been much company. Difficult to live with. It's just that so many things have been pressing against me. Even so the least I can do is act more cheerfully, smile at my wife, think of compliments. I can do that much.

Yes indeed! Regard life as a handful of thistledown, blow on my palm & troubles disappear!

I'm beginning to feel better. Think I'll dust the furniture and then take a walk around the neighborhood.

NOVEMBER 16

Saturday spent alone. B was tutoring from 1 to 3—a boy with long hair and bright eyes who reminds me of a muskrat—then some real-estate agent dropped by so off they went to Marin County. She's planning to buy a piece of ground up there, perhaps enough for a cemetery. At dinner tonight I asked if she'd like to be buried on it. No response, not that I expected much. She's oblivious to all questions outside the boundary of profit. She may be hard of Inner hearing but her eyes are sharp & avid. Dear Bianca. Sweet Bianca.

NOVEMBER 17

She heard me kicking the elevator cage when I came home tonight, greeted me at the door with a suspicious squint. I thought at first she was Aunt Ollie, they smell the same. Lotions of middle age, trailing robes & tissue. Flecks of powder falling on the rug. Anyway, I simply told her I went out for a breath of air. What I'd like to do is find that place again wherever it was—near the women's college I think—take Auntie B along, ring the bell and let her look. Give her a good long look at what I did. She'd never underestimate me again. Ech!—such an idea Earl! Would she be angry with you or not? Impossible to guess. In either case she ought to see what happened.

NOVEMBER 18

Something's dead within me. Ideas that come to me come from the fountainhead of Life, yet when I touch them they're dead. I think about the soft organs of women, it's all I've ever thought about, and their soft cries. How I've wished to hurt them, force them to struggle with their wounds. Make them pay for their brutal insolence toward us—as if we're not worth noticing! How often I've opened a door, stooped for a letter they've dropped, then how was I rewarded? Whenever it happens I turn away without a word and they think it doesn't matter. What if they could read my thoughts? Well, if I don't have very much that's valuable nevertheless I know how to keep my dignity. I'll keep that to the last, without that I might as well stagger around the earth in flapping rags—Earl Summerfield who traded his birthright for—for what? For nothing at all, as far as I can ;ee. Ridicule and contempt. My soul's been sucked up between those oily thighs. Therefore let me weep over myself, Lord, and continue to mourn, for I am greatly embittered in spirit and deeply afflicted. And answer me this, my Lord, such as you are: Why has the capacity for Understanding been given us?

NOVEMBER 19

Tuesday. Rained steadily. Sick at heart. I dread tomorrow.

NOVEMBER 20

Wednesday & strange to say I've been quite alert, not to say efficient. Seldom opened my mouth, refused to talk to anybody during lunch—waving my finger at them to keep silent. Something seems to have happened to my sight enabling me to observe people as though they were reflected in the back of a spoon—thickened lips, eyes bulging, skulls distorted, and so forth. It's really quite strange but I'm not alarmed. I don't believe I'll mention it, merely wait and see. I believe it's a hint of what's to come. Soon perhaps I'll be able to peer through clothing. Discover the bones beneath the flesh. In fact, by developing my faculties I should be able to gaze upon the Ineffable. Others have.

Thread of communion dried & snapped because B knocked at the door, rattled the knob. These hours I spend in solitude affront her & everything that she represents. My indifference bites at her soul. If I'd become enraged, leap from the desk and shout at her, open the door and fight with her—that's exactly what she hopes I'll do. Yes, then she'd feel satisfied. Having had a fight she'd complacently go back to whatever she was doing, but this silence baffles her. I held my breath while she stood just outside the door, picked up the letter opener and tapped that against the globe to let her know she wasn't welcome. Apparently the message wasn't lost, she's retreated and I doubt I'll be bothered for the rest of this evening. It's a mystery to me what she wishes to discuss. The times we argue it seems to me her words are sense-less. It's as if I was listening to the language of some ani-mated little figure in a puppet show. Suppose I put on her hat & coat & reading glasses, plop myself down in her favor-ite chair and see what she says. That might be revealing. If not, no harm done.

Attempting to recall what it was about her that attracted me. Her neatness, yes, the order of her mind. Her quick in-telligence. She's interested in so many things. In fact I do admire her. I always have. I've felt proud to be her husband. Why should such a woman have chosen me? Because I'm utterly undistinguished. Next to me she shines with so much greater brilliance, that's why I've been selected. As to Love —she loves herself. How could I show her that there's no such thing as an ordinary, undistinguished man? No man's undistinguished until he resigns himself to indifference, to commonness, to the death that's always within easy reach.

NOVEMBER 21

My head's packed with notions that might seem unique to other people, remarkable and—well, startling as a play with corpses instead of actors. Yet all things original are both rare and difficult. Primarily it's a matter of inter-pretation. Just the same I think it best to avoid suspicion of what I have in mind, best not to explain. Act naturally. Vla-dimir, for one, has been watching me somewhat more closely than I like. Also, I have a feeling he's talked to others. I've caught him at Fensdeicke's desk, both staring toward me. Small wonder I've been restless. Aside from that, these days are pleasant enough. I'm light on my feet, not in the least fatigued at five o'clock. Walked all the way home this afternoon, which was quite a trip, trotting a few steps now and then. Nearly knocked off my feet at the corner of Arguello although I've got to admit the fault was mine—hurrying across, impatient with the signal. People were shouting at me, however I didn't need them to direct me. I'd like to go back and mimic them. I could—jump up and down, flap my arms. They'd be dumbfounded.

Really as a matter of fact I do feel extraordinarily cheerful! Particularly at this instant! Why? Why? Who cares, I don't. The thing is just that I'm sure the situation will turn out all right. It will. It will because it must. I've been too serious, fret & fret. I'll not behave like that any longer. So much to do. Think about.

Impossible to keep up with my thoughts!—springing about jammed like children on a carrousel. Mirrors spinning, etc.

B pounded on the door—God damn her soul! No matter where I am. No matter what hour of the night. However, she's given up now. I believe I'll read for a few minutes. That usually quiets me. I've been upset. I think it's on account of the news. I alarm myself by listening—waves of awful news wash over me. I don't want to listen, yet how can I stop? At times I've half a mind to wear a helmet. Yes, it may come to that, or jump from the rail of a boat.

Sweet Christ, here I sit! Almost dawn, I'm still here erect as an armored knight from the Middle Ages—Earl Summerfield on a muttering swaybacked horse riding around in the depths of Hell. Clumpety-clump.

NOVEMBER 22

Bought a camera. Stripped away my clothes & took a picture of myself in front of the mirror—stiff as a lance! I'll send her the film. I think she'll like that.

NOVEMBER 23

Saturday & one more week of my life disappeared. Should I be grateful? I suppose I should. It's nearly finished, yet miserably incomplete. Unable to count my blessings, my eyes fill up with tears. At this moment I can't recall my name. Therefore, who am I? Out of the misty past I've come & I am here, yet this is all I ask: Who am I?

NOVEMBER 24

We're created in the shape of hollow vessels into which God pours some measure of Himself, and each time we are emptied He replenishes us—and so until the moment we are broken. But I've poured out myself day after day until there's nobody on earth as empty. There's room enough in me for God to fill, God knows. Why is He elsewhere? Why have I never felt His presence? Have I concealed my heart? What more could I have said? What more could He demand?

NOVEMBER 25

Thirty-six days until this year ends. How awful when we count toward nothing.

NOVEMBER 26

This was Tuesday & I didn't go to the Bureau. Tomorrow there'll be explanations, tonight I won't consider them. I spent most of the day marching back and forth at the edge of the ocean, shoes saturated, face numbed by the roaring wind. I saw the ships that issue from the Golden Gate sail over the horizon to Paradise. I don't think I'll see them return—not that it matters. My life's practically over & I doubt that I regret it. Always I've been turned aside. Long ago I learned to recognize the backs of heads, elbows, heels, the frothy wake of ships. I've wondered if other people feel the same, if they too have felt dismissed. I used to think I'd find out, now I know I won't. Certain secrets are buried with us.

Well, so much for that. I draw myself up in a bucket. Water drips and what did I do this evening? Thought I'd be exhausted by walking along the beach, but no, after supper out again as easily as a leopard. And like a leopard I've grown accustomed to the night. It does seem strange, last year I was more comfortable during the day. Now I'm sure my sight's better after dark. A sliver of moonlight's more than enough. Scudding fog, yards slope away like early burial grounds. And I hear singing—a sound like the rush of water over stones. Accepted by the predatory cats—how often I can see them sitting quietly in the dark. Yes, cats & the rustle of water. Birds motionless on the writhing limbs of trees. One forgets the purpose of fear. History loses meaning. Sooner or later I suppose all of us relive the lives of predecessors.

NOVEMBER 27

This is the final Wednesday of November. Tomorrow the city business stops, tomorrow's Thanksgiving. Thanksgiving! for the mercies of the closing year.

Papers blowing down the windy street. Papers blow along a windy street. Papers blow.

NOVEMBER 28

Opening the Bible to read, shutting it gently, each meditation flows toward another, and yet as I look backward through my life I can't discover the cause of the insidious sweetness that sometimes comes upon me. People around me shake their heads or smile. I feel a need to speak to them, which is why I grope for answers to the questions they would ask, but being as I am, ignorant and less than saintly, not one word rises. So I'm silent & I suppose that's best, standing as I am nearly face to face with Thee.

NOVEMBER 29

Friday & back to work. How separate this day from yesterday. I'd expected, for instance, four full days of solitude. However, the Bureau was open, commerce never ends. Jobs, dollars, men & frogs. What actually are the mercies that we honor? At times like this I decide I must not be human, and whatever's human must be alien to me.

Yes, so it is. Shut out by nature from the usual community. As others fulfill themselves in the company of others so in isolation I'll become Earl Summerfield, not merely a common man who answers to a name. Yes, I don't doubt it can be done. I'll establish the conclusions resulting from my experience, think realistically instead of romantically, challenge conventions, etc. Yet retain mildness of manner, especially when I find myself in an awkward situation, or when I'm dealing with subordinates such as laborers at the Bureau, mechanics, maids, et al. Onus lies in Authority.

To the mirror once again. Why can't I break this habit? I look for my face so often, think that my significance ought to be reflected but there's not much change. I note only that secrecy goes well with my appearance. Rigid pose. I can't say that I'm graceful, but my eyes are black & full of interesting lights. Also I do think that as I've matured my features have acquired—umm, what? Am I more impressive? I've noticed that others stop talking when I approach. And yet few learn from a face what's happening in the deeps of the soul. My perception must be singular, not much escapes me. However as I think about that it's not surprising—no, not at all. Why, compared to me most men are as simple as cattle. All that troubles me, in fact, is that I'm not able to feel certain emotions, ordinary states that others enjoy. Familiar feelings I used to know. Happiness & sorrow. I've lost the power to absorb them.

NOVEMBER 30

So ends the month & leaves a taste of copper on my tongue.

DECEMBER 1

Sunday. My hands and feet are cold, my head drifts 14 inches above its proper place. Seagulls swirl out of the mist like the ghosts of women—silky feathers gleaming, lips opening and shutting as though they mean to attack me. Yes, it's appropriate that this should be Sunday for now I enter upon a life of moral consistency, although with grave consequences to myself.

DECEMBER 2

Cold rain. Ocean squalls. I suppose that soon enough I'll have time for chess and crossword puzzles. More than time enough. Leisure to meditate while others quibble. Let them harangue & dispute, I'll sit and comb my hair as calmly as Peter Brandt, no longer wondering what's best— to be poisoned, hanged, or electrically roasted by the State. I can't see that it's very important. Well, there's one curious thing, our dislike of Blood. No headsman with an ax, as though a bloodless death denies the fact.

Yawning. Must be sleepier than I realize. The room looks luminous, my fingers brilliant, and every thought that comes into my brain seems to be spoken aloud. I get the feeling that I could solve ancient riddles or find mushrooms in the fog. Meanings flash toward me, earth and sky are joined by lightning.

Vision of my own skeleton! Flight. Precognition. Well, maybe I'm soon going to leave the world I've known.

DECEMBER 3

Yes, I'm sure, whatever's been harsh or dissonant about me is dissolving. Last night sat motionless in a ray of moonlight, positive that it signified Rebirth. I know how I've lived. I know how badly, but I know too that I'm no longer what I once was. I see now that we transcend all other life because we, alone, can be aware of life. Life conscious of itself, that must be why we live alone, suffering and then rejoicing as no animals do. God's voice to them is like a whisper in the wilderness, however feeble it sounds to us. Therefore we are confronted by the tragedy of being human —our body imprisoned by commands we are too weak to countermand, our thought at liberty to wander past the outer reaches of the universe. So we exist midway between God and the beasts that He has made & being unable to live alone we commune with both. Freaks, beyond doubt that's what we are, cast out of our first kingdom, devouring animals, birds and fish. No wonder we're lonely, no wonder we are so often terrified.

DECEMBER 4

Wednesday. The rain continues.

This afternoon I went to sleep for a moment while listening to a laborer & had a dream, I think, although I have no idea what it was about. Dreamed I'd gone to sleep on the

Malvern Hills—but don't know where they are, nor what else I dreamed about, except that it was an allegory bearing on the evils of our time. Then I woke up and it seemed to me that my stomach was coated with slime. Strange he didn't notice.

Aside from that—well, not much happened. Gabble of voices like ducks on a lake, and my usual lunch in the basement. Down there I often reflect that I'm a Christian eating bread in a dungeon, unable to look at the sky. However, now it amuses me—I think I could eat paper or buttons, wink back at the flickering tubes of light. I know I'm free. In fact I seldom hear what people say, and such a relief that is! One can be drugged by voices. I used to listen, now I regard human speech as so much rain on the pavement which runs into gutters and is gone. The desires and achievements of other people no longer interest me because I've lost the urge to struggle. The result would be predictable. Not that I doubt my ability or my strength, simply that I could stoop down and write a message on the floor: The applause of 200 million is not so splendid as Ambition would have us think. So, when Vladimir and McAuliffe talk I pretend to listen, but actually I don't. What seems to them of terrible importance seems to me no more significant than the tufts on a quilt. When they talk directly to me I examine my hands.

DECEMBER 5

Decided not to go to work today. Telephoned, reported myself sick. Didn't eat. Sat on the fire escape most of the afternoon waiting for sunset, anxious for shadows to mask the hillside. Only then did I begin to feel alive. Daylight wastes me. I'm not much use while the sun is visible, in fact I feel very much like a candle. Sitting on those iron rungs, swaying back and forth, waving to passers-by. How

THE DIARY OF A RAPIST

small & futile they appeared. How could anyone fail to pity them as they walk with such alacrity through the mills of Death! Aware of no presence but their own, thick with a passion for cruel deeds, how could they learn what I have learned? Who could point out to them that if they waited quietly at home there'd be no evil anywhere on earth. Who can show them that the striations of a fingernail are of greater portent than any chancellor's decision. Wait at home—that's what I'd tell them if they'd listen. Wait without moving, only then is glory manifest. Wait for what is to be.

Well, I suppose that for the sake of ordinary Health I ought to go into the kitchen. Yes, I should eat. In a little while I will but right now am reluctant to interfere with the chain of my thought—I see it stretching brighter than a chain of diamonds across some frightful abyss.

DECEMBER 6

Friday. I returned to the office, did my work without complaint, greeted them all & told them I'd recovered. A temporary indisposition is what I said & they smiled & I smiled. Obviously I could go on and on like this. At five o'clock I walked down Market Street to look at the people buying gifts, the sight astounded me. There should be no gifts exchanged. Christmas Day is one day we should spend on our knees, a moment when all of us ought to reveal to others the innermost substance of the heart. Yes, then there would be such a fund of love that the worship of everything else would crumble. How long—how long until this happens? I sit here listening but I hear only a vast promise of destruction. Conquest, Slaughter, Famine & Death! Galloping toward us I behold the four horsemen of the Apoca-

244

lypse. Therefore, who should be amazed that I've done what I have done? Who could possibly be amazed?

DECEMBER 7

Half minded to kill myself, otherwise I'll spend these last few nights as I've spent others—locked in, determined that nothing shall keep me from my notes. Yet what's accomplished?

Sick with my own importance I go on and on like a musician who's never satisfied but continues stringing and unstringing his instrument.

DECEMBER 8

Not much sleep last night. Did I sleep at all? I didn't leave the room. Or did I? Just before dawn I lay down on the floor & shut my eyes—I remember rolling across the rug, then morning surprised me chewing on a towel. I must have slept. Whether or not, yesterday's come and gone—so fast. So fast! Each day moves like a locust's wing & there's no mercy.

Could it be that because we are born in misery we spend our lives in such a futile search?

DECEMBER 9

Monday, to work. These last few days I've felt distraught. Could it be the approach of Christmas? Gilded cardboard ornaments sway in every street, recorded carols attempt to reassure us. Who now believes them? O Come All

245

Ye Faithful! O Come Ye! Why? Who can answer? The Pope in Rome reminds us of certain blessings, I say so what! Design another Zodiac. I've seen what I didn't know before, heard much I never understood. This morning a new and eloquent corpse was discovered in the park close to the Academy of Sciences, intestines looped over the boughs of an evergreen tree as though it was a primitive sacrifice. Thus we continue, scurrying through a German forest.

I walked to the corner of Geary a few minutes ago. There I bent down and wrote a message with my finger in the middle of the street: Save Us!

DECEMBER 10

Yes, the hour's near at hand, the hold is loose, signs multiply, all things turn to barrenness. Wrongdoing shall be written of those who have done it. The age that now is passing shall be sealed, great books gradually open against the firmament. Infants one year old shall speak, sown ground will not yield, friends destroy each other, roses wither.

DECEMBER 11

Whatever I used to be I am not now. Whatever I was has darkened & shriveled into a lump of slag. I feel as weightless and porous as a piece of lava.

DECEMBER 12

Pondering little more of earth, I wait. Shall I wait much longer? Down the street the wind blows & the wind blows & paper bells are torn apart.

246

DECEMBER 13

Grateful for this night during which there was no Interruption. Grateful for the utter silence that encloses me —I've painted a story on the walls and ceiling of my room. Nobody else has seen it but the significance is clear: We have underestimated the nature of Man.

Yes, circles & crosses, conduits of beneficence join. Thus the mind arrives at the desired conclusion.

DECEMBER 14

They say that whoever talks about and reflects upon some wicked thing he has done is thinking the vileness again because we are caught in what we think—with the entire soul are we caught in this, so we still are caught in vileness. Nor can the spirit turn away, nor the heart fail to rot. But I say this is false & the choice is mine. I also say that it makes no difference whether I accuse myself or allow others to accuse me, for if I find myself guilty then I am obligated to punish myself. If others find me guilty they may do the same, but their power is less than mine so that whatever they do is absurd. I also say that I am responsible for what I've done. Either that or we live beneath the shield of an inverted God.

DECEMBER 15

Man turned beast becomes His opposite.

DECEMBER 16

The shedding of blood ends in Death but the fountain of semen is Life. A voice from ages past calls to me: Watchman, what of the night?

DECEMBER 17

Folly, falsehood, hatred & malice! Heaven and earth in little space. Blackness, blackness.

Fire streams from my fingertips—I see a crowd of struggling figures. I could perform miracles to astound them, but what would be the use? Say that I chose to feed them, soon they'd be hungry. Or if I gave them water and wine to drink they'd be thirsty before their lips were dry. Nothing calms them, nothing appeases them, yet they believe their lives are worthwhile. If the ocean rose above the shore each would cry out that He should be saved. I know better. I know better because I look down on them from a great distance—from such a distance that their features cannot be distinguished. I find very little to choose among them. Very little indeed. Misery of flesh and blood. Let them walk the path their fathers walked because they cannot find another. Let them walk in that direction until they pause, until they hesitate & discover among themselves that they are wondering. And let their first questions reveal to them the direction they have taken as well as where it ends.

Yes, it's in the asking of many questions that we find out what we are.

DECEMBER

DECEMBER 18

Wednesday & this week soon over. Presently the month, presently the year. Should I care what becomes of me? Should I ask who pays attention to the rattle of seeds in a gourd? Next year at this time who's going to ask what became of Summerfield? Well, one or two. Even so, I think I've learned much in life and therefore I believe I'll learn at least as much in death. I see now that I've invited Death by the error of my life. I'm ready to hold out my hands. I may be innocent of evil, if there's no act of evil without a guilty mind, yet how to say this and still retain my dignity? —there's not much else to hope for.

And when the rest of it is over & each mind has been made up, what then? Sometimes the curtain falls while the play continues.

DECEMBER 19

The most difficult thing will be to explain—to tell her how I felt. How can I let her know that I was terrified of life, and this was the reason I fell in love with hate? How can I help her to understand?

I pretended to myself that somehow she might love me because she is what I loved, and all that I've ever loved, all that I ever could love. I persuaded myself that she was frightened only by the depth of her own feeling toward me —saying what I needed to hear. But she does hate me & hopes for nothing so much as my death, I do know that. I wanted her more than I could want a basket of blue diamonds, or the softest yellowest bolt of silk in Japan. Blessings came to me from the blessing of her body & beside her a

249

silver statue of the Virgin would look like a monstrous idol of gilded clay. Intercourse with her had no bitterness, so I think living with her would have no grief. I'd give anything to grow old with her, but I'll sooner hear snow falling on a mountain.

Why is it, I wonder, that we're able to let go of all things and desire only one woman so that we follow and stare at her and reach for her in our sleep? Why is she worth so much? Judith the daughter of Merari made Holofernes faint with the beauty of her face. She put on a linen dress to deceive him, arranged her hair and spread ointment on her eyes & showed him her sandals, and then she passed the scimitar through his neck as though he was an ox to be sacrificed. This is what I wonder, and all I know is that together we form a pattern of marvelous subtility.

DECEMBER 20

Five days until Christmas, then I'll go. Why should I be afraid? I may not die in vain.

DECEMBER 21

Who does not enter into the generations of Man?

DECEMBER 22

I called & told her that on Christmas morning I'd knock at the door. Drunk with the joy of telling I promised that I'd bow down in front of her and ask to be forgiven. Yet I doubt that I can bow low enough—my deepest obeisance is pitiful.

DECEMBER 23

Morning, noon, finally this evening. I believe that only among shadows have I grown visible in my glory. By daylight I think I would save myself from the ignorance, from the violence, from the limitless hypocrisy upon which we are founded. Morning, noon & finally the border of eternity past which there's neither hope, despair, nor happiness, beyond which nothing exists and nothing dissolves. When the ashes of my body have been scattered there will be people who say I've gone, but I will be among them—listening as they talk. Let them protest, I will be here.

DECEMBER 24

Now weigh me a weight of fire, measure me a measure of wind, call back a single day that has passed. Leaf of a green plant, touch of a child's hand. So enters the darkness, so helpless are we.

DECEMBER 25

In the sight of our Lord I must be one of many.

DECEMBER 26

DECEMBER 27

THE DIARY OF A RAPIST

DECEMBER 28

DECEMBER 29

DECEMBER 30

DECEMBER 31